EXPERIENCE & EVENT DESIGN
2025/2026

EXPERIENCE & EVENT DESIGN
2025/2026

Katharina Stein

avedition

INHALT
CONTENTS

ayscan *In den digitalen Raum mit ayscan: Unter www.ayscan.de herunterladen, den Anweisungen folgen und die mit Symbol versehenen Seiten um Bild, Film und Ton erweitern. Viel Spaß! Enter digital space with ayscan: Download at www.ayscan.de, follow the instructions and scan pages marked with the symbol to enjoy additional photos, films and sounds. Have fun!*

Die Zeiten sind schwierig – wirtschaftlich, gesellschaftlich und geopolitisch. Die Zukunft ist ungewiss, Budgets schrumpfen, Investitionen stocken. Das bekommt auch die Live-Kommunikation zu spüren.

Seit etwas weniger als einem Jahr verzeichnet der ifo-Geschäftsklimaindex der Veranstaltungsbranche mit ca. 9.000 monatlichen Meldungen einen stetigen Abwärtstrend. Geschäftsklima und der Auftragsbestand bewegen sich dauerhaft im zweistelligen Minusbereich. Einzig die Preisentwicklung bleibt stabil positiv. Gestiegene Kosten und Inflation sind zweifellos zwei Treiber dieser Entwicklung. Hinzu kommen politische Entwicklungen, die die Wirtschaft verunsichern. Faschistische und rechtspopulistische Strömungen nehmen in vielen Ländern beängstigend schnell zu – schüren Hass, Angst und Hetze, möchten kulturelle und nachhaltige Fortschritte zurückdrehen und setzen mit nationalen Abschottungsstrategien die globale Wirtschaft unter Druck.

Das trifft eine Branche wie unsere ganz direkt. Schließlich leben wir von einer freien, kreativen Kultur, innovativen Firmen und Menschen aus aller Welt. Kulturabbau, Ausgrenzung und wirtschaftliche oder ideologische Beschränkungen treffen uns im Kern unserer Arbeit.

GERADE DESHALB SIND WIR JETZT GEFRAGT, DAGEGEN AUFZUSTEHEN.

„Und die Kommunikationsbranche kann bzw. könnte deutlich dazu beitragen, entschieden dagegen vorzugehen. Sie verfügt über die notwendigen Werkzeuge, das Netzwerk und die Fähigkeiten, wirkungsvoll zu kommunizieren", betont Arne Heyen vom Zentrum für Politische Schönheit. Im Kurzinterview (S. 150) spricht er unter anderem darüber, welche Kraft Erlebnisdesign als Protestform hat.

Darüber hinaus sind Erlebnisse gerade in Krisenzeiten von unschätzbarem Wert. Sie stiften Gemeinschaft, stärken Vertrauen und geben Zuversicht. Sie eröffnen Räume für neue Perspektiven, für Inspiration und ermöglichen den kurzen Ausbruch aus dem Alltag.

Erfreulicherweise entstehen solche Momente auch weiterhin. Auffällig ist dabei die Rolle neuer Technologien. Sie sind fester Bestandteil heutiger Erlebnisdesigns – sie erweitern die kreativen, interaktiven und individuellen Möglichkeiten und lassen außergewöhnliche Erlebnisse entstehen.

Gleichzeitig gilt: Technologie soll dem Erlebnis dienen, nicht es dominieren. „Wirklich gute Erlebnisse leben vom Erlebnis, nicht von den neuesten Technologien!", sagt Sören Fricke von SOLIDSENSE. Andererseits weiß Christoph Diederichs von Atelier Markgraph: „Manchmal ist es eine neue [...] Technologie, die den Zugang zu einem Thema überhaupt erst interessant macht". Die Herausforderung liegt im ausgewogenen Einsatz – zwischen Trend und Mehrwert.

Erlebnisorientierte Technologien müssen heute vieles leisten: Sie sollen Inhalte tragen, Aufmerksamkeit erzeugen, emotional berühren, leichte und multisensorische Zugänge eröffnen, wirtschaftlich bleiben, nachhaltigen Kriterien genügen und gleichzeitig kritisch hinterfragt werden. Im Interview berichten Atelier Markgraph und SOLIDSENSE über Potenziale und Grenzen, Innovationen und Erfolgsfaktoren neuer Technologien (S. 8).

Zeitgenössische Beispiele zeigt diese Ausgabe. Auch wenn die aktuelle Lage in diesem Jahrbuch spürbar ist und es weniger Projekte als sonst präsentiert, bleibt eines deutlich: Mit ästhetischen Raumerlebnissen, gemeinschaftsstiftenden Events und immersiven Welten demonstrieren sie den bleibenden Wert von Live-Kommunikation.

Auf geht's – zum Stöbern, Diskutieren und Demonstrieren!

ZWISCHEN KRISE UND KREATIVITÄT
BETWEEN CRISIS AND CREATIVITY
INTRODUCTION BY KATHARINA STEIN

We are facing difficult times – in terms of economics, society and geopolitics. The future is uncertain, budgets are dwindling, investments are stagnating. This is also having an impact on live communication.

For about a year, the ifo business climate index for the events industry has been indicating a constant downward trend with around 9000 monthly announcements. The business climate and the order status are constantly within a two-figure minus range. It is only the price development that is seeing a stable increase. A rise in costs and inflation are no doubt two drivers of this development. In addition, the economy is destabilised by political developments. Fascist and right-wing populist movements are gaining importance at a frightening rate in many countries – fuelling hate, fear and agitation, seeking to curb cultural and lasting progress, and are exerting pressure on the global economy with national isolation strategies.

This has direct consequences for a sector such as ours. After all, we are dependent on a free, creative culture, with innovative companies and people from around the world. Cultural depletion, exclusion and economic or ideological restrictions hit the core of our work.

THIS IS PRECISELY WHY WE ARE NOW CALLED UPON TO TAKE A STAND AGAINST THIS.

"And the communications sector can or could contribute significantly to taking decisive action against it. It has the necessary tools, the network and the capabilities to communicate effectively," Arne Heyen from the organisation Political Beauty emphasises. In a brief interview (p. 150), he talks amongst other things about what power experience design has as a form of protest.

In addition, experiences are of inestimable value especially in times of crisis. They forge a sense of community, strengthen trust and foster optimism. They widen the scope for new perspectives, for inspiration and enable entertaining escapes from everyday life.

Fortunately, such moments continue to be created, with new technologies playing a notable role. They are a firm component of current experience design – they widen the scope of creative, interactive and individual possibilities and result in exceptional experiences.

At the same time, technology should serve the experience and not dominate it. "Really good experiences are driven by the experience, not by the latest technologies!" says Sören Fricke from SOLIDSENSE. On the other hand, Christoph Diederichs from Atelier Markgraph states: "Sometimes it is a new technology [...] that provides an interesting avenue for broaching a topic." The challenge lies in finding a balance between trend and added value.

Experience-orientated technologies need to meet a lot of requirements today: They should support content, generate attention, be emotionally moving, provide multisensory experiences, maintain profitability, meet sustainability criteria and at the same time be critically questioned. In our interview, Atelier Markgraph and SOLIDSENSE report about potential and limitations, innovations and success factors of new technologies (p. 8).

This edition shows contemporary examples. Even if the current situation is evident in this yearbook and it presents fewer projects than usual, one thing remains clear: With aesthetic spatial experiences, community-forging events and immersive worlds, they demonstrate the ongoing value of live communication.

Get stuck in – browse, discuss and take a stand!

Neue Technologien sind ein fester Bestandteil des Erlebnisdesigns. Doch wie stellt ihr im Prozess sicher, dass nicht die Technik, sondern der Mensch und das Erlebnis im Mittelpunkt stehen? Und welche typischen Fehler gilt es zu vermeiden?

Christoph Diederichs, Atelier Markgraph:

Wichtig für uns ist es, neue Technologien nicht als Selbstzweck einzusetzen, sondern um ein Erlebnis zu bereichern oder zu intensivieren. Oft bieten sich ganz neue Möglichkeiten, die ohne diese Technologie zu umständlich oder gar nicht realisierbar wären. Dabei sollte man aber nicht zu dogmatisch sein und formatoffen in die Ideenfindung gehen. Digitale Lösungen sind nicht automatisch immer die beste Option. Doch manchmal ist es eine neue, für Besucher:innen möglicherweise noch unbekannte Technologie, die den Zugang zu einem Thema überhaupt erst interessant macht.

Für uns als Fachleute sind neue Technologien meist intuitiv und einfach in der Bedienung – Besuchende, die das Konzept oder die Technologie aber nicht kennen, stehen vielleicht mit einem Fragezeichen vor der Anwendung oder lassen sie im schlimmsten Fall unbeachtet. Daher muss der Zugang so einfach und intuitiv wie möglich gestaltet sein. In manchen Fällen gelingt das auch nur mit entsprechend geschultem Personal, das die User bei der Experience begleitet.

Photo: Axl Jansen

Christoph Diederichs,
Management Digital & Interactive at Atelier Markgraph

Wir haben bei Atelier Markgraph eine eigene Abteilung für genau diese Fragestellungen und die meisten unserer Experience-Designer:innen haben einen Hintergrund im Bereich Human Interaction und Experience Design – da steht der Mensch per se an erster Stelle.

Sören Fricke, SOLIDSENSE:

WIRKLICH GUTE ERLEBNISSE LEBEN VOM ERLEBNIS, NICHT VON DEN NEUESTEN TECHNOLOGIEN!

Das ist auf den ersten Blick so banal, manchmal aber schwer tatsächlich umzusetzen: Es gilt immer erst Inhalt, Didaktik und die Besucherführung zu erarbeiten, bevor man in das technische Design oder gar überhaupt irgendeinen Gestaltungsprozess einsteigt. Wenn dann mit dem Design begonnen wird, darf eine „fancy" neue Technologie niemals um ihrer selbst willen vorgesehen sein, sondern muss vielmehr immer ebendiesen Vorgaben untergeordnet werden.

Emotionen sind der Kern aller Erlebnisse. Welche Technologien und Anwendungsszenarien bieten neue Möglichkeiten, die gerade emotionale Reaktionen verstärken können?

Sören Fricke: „Das Neue" ist immer etwas, was Emotionen auslöst. Zugleich darf dieses Neue aber nicht abschreckend oder einschüchternd sein, es muss im besten Fall einfach so passieren, sprich, Nutzer:innen sollen erst mittendrin bemerken, dass hier etwas Überraschendes, Neues geschieht. Ähnlich wie bei der Technologie ist das Neue nur Mittel zum Zweck, nicht der Zweck selbst!

TECHNOLOGIEN – EMOTIONEN AUS DEM HINTERGRUND
TECHNOLOGIES – EMOTIONS FROM THE BACKGROUND
INTERVIEW WITH CHRISTOPH DIEDERICHS (ATELIER MARKGRAPH); SÖREN FRICKE (SOLIDSENSE)

New technologies are a consistent feature of experience design. But how do you ensure in the process that the focus is not on technology but on people and the experience? And what typical errors need to be avoided?

Christoph Diederichs, Atelier Markgraph:

It is important that we don't use new technology as an end in itself but to enrich or intensify an experience. Completely new possibilities often present themselves that would be too difficult or not practicable at all without this technology. But one should not be too dogmatic and go into the brainstorming with an open mind when it comes to formats. Digital solutions are not automatically always the best option. But sometimes it is a new technology, which visitors may still be unfamiliar with, that provides an interesting avenue for broaching a topic.

For us as experts, new technologies are usually intuitive and easy to use – while visitors who are not familiar with the concept or the technology may struggle to use it and in the worst case pass it by. Access must therefore be as straightforward and intuitive as possible. In some cases, this is only possible with suitably trained personnel who accompany the users during the experience.

At Atelier Markgraph, we have a designated department for precisely these matters and most of our experience designers have a background in the field of Human Interaction and Experience Design – where the focus is on people per se.

Sören Fricke, SOLIDSENSE:

REALLY GOOD EXPERIENCES ARE DRIVEN BY THE EXPERIENCE, NOT BY THE LATEST TECHNOLOGIES!

Photo: Markus Burkhardt Fotografie

Sören Fricke,
Managing Director at SOLIDSENSE

This seems obvious at first glance but sometimes it can in fact be difficult to put into practice: the first step is always to work out the content, didactics and user journey, before embarking on the technical design or any other design process. When starting on the design, a "fancy" new technology may never be considered because of itself but rather must always be secondary to the overall purpose.

Emotions are at the heart of all experiences. What technologies and usage scenarios offer new possibilities that can reinforce emotional reactions in particular?

Sören Fricke: "Novelty" is always something that triggers emotions. At the same time, however, this novelty must not be daunting or overwhelming, the best-case scenario is for it just to happen, so that users only notice underway that something surprising and new is happening. Just like technology, novelty should only serve a purpose, not be the purpose in itself!

Christoph Diederichs: Für mich sind das zwei Dinge: Zum einen sollten Erlebnisse, wenn möglich, als Gruppenerlebnisse gedacht werden.

ES MACHT EINFACH DEUTLICH MEHR SPASS, DINGE GEMEINSAM ZU ERLEBEN.

In Gruppen können außerdem komplett neue Arten der Interaktion entstehen, die unter Umständen vorher gar nicht so konzipiert waren, jedoch eine große Bereicherung für die Experience darstellen.

Der zweite Aspekt ist die Einzigartigkeit des Erlebnisses. Besonders jüngeres Publikum ist durch Smartphone und Computer verwöhnt und nicht gerade leicht zu begeistern. Ein gutes Beispiel dafür ist der von uns konzipierte Boxenstopp-Bereich im Mercedes-Benz Museum. Wo sonst hat man die Möglichkeit, ein Thema in einer derartigen Tiefe zu erleben? Die Rennstrategie mit Reifenwahl, Boxenstopps etc. betrachten wir in der Formel 1 in der Regel nur als Beobachter, nicht jedoch als Agierende innerhalb einer Gruppe.

Einzigartige immersive Technologien sind kostenintensiv. Können auch Unternehmen mit begrenzten Budgets sinnvolle technikgestützte Erlebnisse schaffen?

Christoph Diederichs: Begrenzte Budgets schärfen den Fokus. Oft ist die Technologie gar nicht der größte Kostentreiber, es sind eher die Erstellung des Konzepts und die Abstimmungen darüber. Besteht kundenseitig eine klare Strategie und abgestimmte Inhalte, macht das die Erstellung der Erlebnisse in der Regel günstiger.

In der Praxis ist dies jedoch selten gegeben bzw. ist es oftmals auch sinnvoll, die Strategie und das Konzept gemeinsam zu entwickeln.

Gerade AR-Erlebnisse lassen sich durch moderne Entwicklungsmethoden und Tools mittlerweile recht effizient umsetzen. Mit No-Code-Software können auch Nichtprogrammierer:innen eigene Cases erstellen oder zumindest anpassen, ohne dass jedes Mal eine neue Softwareentwicklung benötigt wird. Ansonsten kann ein Ansatz sein, auf bereits entwickelte Module oder Konzepte zurückzugreifen oder Existierendes geschickt zu kombinieren. Nicht immer muss das Rad neu erfunden werden.

Sören Fricke: Immersivität ist zudem ein Buzzword und wird leider inzwischen mit einem technologisch aufwendigen Erlebnis gleichgesetzt, meint aber ja etwas ganz anderes: nämlich ein Erlebnis, in das ich kognitiv voll eintauche, darin mitspiele.

Dafür braucht es weder Technologie, also Technik, noch erfordert es die großen Budgets, um Erlebnisse immersiv und nachhaltig zu gestalten. Benötigt werden schlicht der Fokus auf die Zielgruppe und die direkte Erfüllung ihrer Erwartungen. Nicht immer ist der Einsatz von Technik der richtige Weg zu einem tollen Erlebnis. Manchmal sind es auch nur die einfache Umsetzung und ein direkter Zugang ohne Hemmschwellen.

Wie bedeutend ist das Zusammenspiel von physischen und digitalen Erlebnissen dabei? Und worauf kommt es an, sodass eine ganzheitliche Erfahrung entsteht?

Sören Fricke: Rein digitale Erlebnisse im Raum sind nicht mehr zeitgemäß. Was wirklich aufmerksam macht und in Erinnerung bleibt, sind selbst die kleinsten physischen Interaktionen, die mit digitaler Content-Tiefe angereichert werden. Auf diese Art werden mehr Sinne angesprochen und das Erlebnis wird zugleich sowohl dem menschlichen Spieltrieb als auch der gewünschten inhaltlichen Kommunikation gerecht.

Christoph Diederichs: Ich empfinde es immer als spannende Herausforderung, Physisches und Digitales miteinander zu verbinden, denn so schöpft man das Beste aus beiden Welten. Es darf gern mal das rein digitale Erlebnis oder das rein analoge Exponat sein – auch das kann beindrucken! Aber wenn beides elegant miteinander verbunden wird, entsteht einfach am meisten Spaß.

Christoph Diederichs: For me there are two things to take into consideration. Firstly, experiences should be conceived wherever possible as group experiences.

IT IS SIMPLY A LOT MORE FUN TO EXPERIENCE THINGS TOGETHER.

Groups can also prompt completely new ways of interacting, which may not have been thought of beforehand but represents a significant enrichment for the experience.

The second aspect is the uniqueness of the experience. The younger public, in particular, has been spoilt by smartphones and computers and isn't exactly easy to enthuse. A good example of this is the pit stop area at the Mercedes-Benz Museum that we designed. Where else does one have the possibility to experience a topic in such depth? We normally only watch the race strategy with the choice of tyres, pit stops etc. as an observer, but not as an active member of a group.

Unique immersive technologies are costly. Can companies with limited budgets create meaningful experiences supported by technology nonetheless?

Christoph Diederichs: Limited budgets sharpen one's focus. Often the biggest driver of costs is not the technology but rather creating the concept and negotiations about it. If there is a clear strategy on the part of the customer and the content has been set, it usually makes creating the experiences cheaper.

In practice, however, this is rarely the case and it often also makes sense to develop the strategy and the concept together.

AR experiences, in particular, can now be realised quite efficiently through modern development methods and tools. Even non-programmers can create or at least adjust their own cases using no-code software, without a new software development being needed every time. Another approach could be to make use of already developed modules or concepts or to cleverly combine what already exists. It is not necessary to keep reinventing the wheel.

Sören Fricke: Immersivity is a buzzword and is unfortunately equated nowadays with a technologically sophisticated experience, but it means something quite different: namely an experience that one fully immerses in cognitively, takes part in.

It requires neither technology nor big budgets to design immersive and lasting experiences. All that is needed is simply a focus on the target group and the direct fulfilment of their expectations. The use of technology is not always the right path to a great experience. Sometimes it is also just the simple execution and direct access without thresholds.

How important is the interplay of physical and digital experiences in this? And what is key for creating an immersive experience?

Sören Fricke: Purely digital spatial experiences are no longer state of the art. What really draws attention and remains memorable are even just the smallest physical interactions that are enriched with digital content depth. This appeals to more of the senses and the experience addresses the human playful spirit while at the same time meeting the content communication requirements.

Christoph Diederichs: I always find it is an interesting challenge to combine the physical and the digital, as it brings forth the best of both worlds. Sometimes it can be a purely digital experience or a purely analogue one – these can also be impressive! But when both are combined elegantly it simply results in the most fun.

Sowohl hybride als auch rein digitale Erlebnisse haben einen entscheidenden Vorteil: Die informative Tiefe ist leicht skalierbar.

Welche Bedeutung haben haptisches Feedback und multisensorische Gestaltung in diesem Kontext?

Christoph Diederichs: Eine große! Wir wollen Erlebnisse schaffen, an denen ich nicht zu Hause mit meinem Smartphone oder per Computer partizipieren kann, sondern nur an diesem einen bestimmten Ort, in diesem Moment. Das macht den Ort und das Erlebnis einzigartig.

Sören Fricke: Haptisches oder auch auditives Feedback sind eine wunderbare Möglichkeit, ein Erlebnis kognitiv ganzheitlicher werden zu lassen. Die Ansprache zusätzlicher menschlicher Sinne verankert ein Erlebnis tiefer in der Erinnerung. Tatsächlich lässt sich hier am User Interface aktueller Smartphones sehr gut ableiten, wie es richtig gemacht wird. Grundsätzlich aber ist der gemischte Einsatz von physischer Interaktion (die über den Touch auf einem Monitor hinausgeht) immer ein Erfolgsgarant, sofern dieser selbsterklärend und für die Zielgruppe barrierefrei gestaltet ist.

KI ist ein allgegenwärtiges Thema. Welche konkreten und gewinnbringenden Einsatzmöglichkeiten seht ihr für sie im Erlebnisdesign? In welchen Bereichen kann sie die Branche am stärksten verändern? Und wo seht ihr kritische Herausforderungen oder Grenzen?

Christoph Diederichs: Bisher betrachten wir KI mit positivem Interesse, sehen jedoch auch die kritischen Seiten, zum Beispiel die benötigte Energie und auch die möglichen Auswirkungen auf die Kreativbranche. Unser Berufsfeld lebt von Storywritern, Programmierern, Voice Actors und Gestaltern. Dieses Feld der KI zu überlassen entspricht nicht unserem kreativen Anspruch und Selbstverständnis. Das heißt nicht, dass wir KI nicht gezielt einsetzen. Wir nutzen sie beispielsweise für Visualisierungen oder um Inhalte zusammenzufassen.

LETZTLICH GIBT UNS KI DIE MÖGLICHKEIT, UNSERE ARBEIT EFFIZIENTER ZU MACHEN. WIR SEHEN SIE ABER DEFINITIV NICHT ALS DIE LÖSUNG FÜR ALLES.

Interessant ist der Einsatz von generativer KI in Erlebnissen dann, wenn Besuchende plötzlich nicht mehr nur vordefinierten Content erleben, sondern dieser sich individuell je nach Nutzer selbst entwickelt und verändert. Das bietet eine ganz neue Denkweise für Erlebnisse. Diesen Ansatz verproben wir auch bereits in ersten Umsetzungen.

Sören Fricke: Hierüber könnte man wohl Seiten schreiben. KI ermöglicht es, ohne großen Aufwand individuell zugeschnittene Interaktionen und Erlebnisse zu kreieren – Stichwort: User-Centered Experience Design.

Hierzu fehlt aber oftmals die Datenbasis. Viele Kunden sind sich über ihre Besucherschaft gar nicht genau genug im Klaren und haben daher wiederum ihre Inhalte auch nicht für verschiedene Usergruppen optimiert.

Die größte Veränderung ist in den digitalen oder physisch-digital gemischten Erlebnissen zu erwarten. Webseiten mit einer starren Navigation wird es nicht mehr geben, diese werden zukünftig individuell „on the fly" für User:innen aus einem Contentpool erstellt werden. Mit Touchanwendungen auf Messeständen, in Showrooms und Museen wird es sich ähnlich verhalten.

Die größte Herausforderung hierbei wird sein, die Denkweisen in der inhaltlichen Zusammenstellung des Contents anzupassen, weg von der Linearität und hin zum KI-kuratierten Schwarmwissen.

Both hybrid and purely digital experiences have a decisive advantage: the informative depth can be easily adjusted.

What importance do haptic feedback and multisensory design have in this context?

Christoph Diederichs: Great importance! We want to create experiences that one cannot participate in at home with a smartphone or computer, instead only at this particular place, at this moment. This makes the place and the experience unique.

Sören Fricke: Haptic or auditory feedback are a wonderful way of making an experience more cognitively immersive. Appealing to additional human senses anchors an experience deeper in the memory. You can actually see on the user interface of current smartphones how to do it right. In principle though, the mixed use of physical interaction (that goes beyond the touch on a monitor) is always a guarantee for success, insofar as it must be self-explanatory and is designed barrier-free for the target group.

AI is widely discussed. What concrete and advantageous usage possibilities do you see for it in experience design? In what areas can it change the sector the most? And where do you see critical challenges or limitations?

Christoph Diederichs: Until now we have viewed AI with positive interest, but we are also aware of the critical aspects such as the required energy and the possible effects on the creative industry. Our professional field requires story writers, programmers, voice actors and designers. Handing this field over to AI is not in the interests of our creative ambitions and self-understanding. This does not mean that we don't use AI in a targeted manner. We use it, for visualisations or for summarising content.

ULTIMATELY, AI ENABLES US TO MAKE OUR WORK MORE EFFICIENT. HOWEVER, WE DEFINITELY DON'T SEE IT AS THE SOLUTION TO EVERYTHING.

The use of generative AI for experiences is of interest if visitors suddenly experience not only predefined content anymore but instead it evolves and changes individually according to the user. This offers a completely new way of thinking for experiences. We are already trying out this approach in initial realisations.

Sören Fricke: One could no doubt write pages about this. AI makes it possible to create individually tailored interactions and experiences without great effort. Keyword: user-centred experience design.

However, the data basis for this is often lacking. Many customers do not have a sufficient understanding of their visitors and have therefore not optimised their content for various user groups.

The biggest change is to be expected in digital or mixed physical-digital experiences. There will no longer be websites with rigid navigation, in future they will be created individually for users "on the fly" from a content pool. It will be similar for touch applications at exhibition stands, in showrooms and museums.

The greatest challenge will be to shift ways of thinking when compiling the content, away from linearity and towards AI-curated swarm intelligence.

Nachhaltigkeit ist ein ebenso großes Thema. Technologien können dabei helfen, nachhaltige Lösungen zu entwickeln. Gleichzeitig verbrauchen sie eine Menge Ressourcen – gerade die derzeit beliebten KIs. Wie geht ihr mit diesem Widerspruch um?

Sören Fricke: Die Experience-Branche mit Messen, Events und einem Fokus auf dem Moment steht natürlich vor einer großen Herausforderung in puncto Nachhaltigkeit, insbesondere in der ökologischen Bedeutung des Wortes. Vor allem sollten Projekte im Sinn ihres Lifecycles betrachtet werden. Muss etwas nur für diesen einen Moment kreiert werden oder kann es auch für mehr als einen Moment dienen? Gibt es vielleicht andere Mittel, das gewünschte Ziel zu erreichen, die weniger Ressourcen abfordern? Kann vielleicht gar das Ziel angepasst werden, um etwas Langfristigeres oder weniger Ressourcenintensives zu entwickeln?

Christoph Diederichs: Unsere Erfahrung zeigt, dass interaktive Erlebnisse eine recht lange Halbwertszeit haben. Das sollte man bei der Zielsetzung, bei der Entwicklung des Konzepts und auch bei der Realisierung berücksichtigen. Die Anwendung sollte dann eben nicht nur bei einer einzigen Veranstaltung zum Einsatz kommen, sondern kontinuierlich über mehrere Jahre verwendet werden – Software lässt sich bekanntermaßen ja gut weiterentwickeln und aktualisieren.

Ein kleiner Blick in die Zukunft: Welche aktuellen Projekte, Forschungsprojekte oder experimentellen Technologien beobachtet ihr mit besonderem Interesse?

Christoph Diederichs: Wir warten noch auf eine marktreife AR-Brille, die für Endkunden erschwinglich ist und weniger als 300 Gramm wiegt. Besonders spannend sind auch Hologramme oder 3D-Displays, die ohne Brille auskommen. Im VR-Bereich tut sich was mit der Bigscreen Beyond 2 – insbesondere im Bereich Minimierung und Gewichtsreduktion. Außerdem beobachten wir Konferenzen wie zum Beispiel die SIGGRAPH immer mit Spannung – dort werden interessante Paper oder Produkte vorgestellt.

Sören Fricke: Im Grunde gibt es für uns gerade nichts, was da deutlich heraussticht. Vielleicht kann man noch die immer umfangreicher verfügbaren transparenten Videoflächen nennen, sei es nun als LED oder auch OLED. Die Möglichkeiten, die der Blick auf das „Dahinter" mit der Möglichkeit von Kommunikation auf dem transparenten Layer davor eröffnet, sind sicher noch nicht ausgeschöpft.

Technologische Möglichkeiten entwickeln sich rasant – von VR, AR und MR über interaktive Trackingsysteme bis hin zu künstlicher Intelligenz. Welche Entwicklungen oder Technologien haben aus eurer Sicht aktuell den größten Einfluss auf das Erlebnisdesign? Und warum?

Christoph Diederichs:

AUGMENTED-REALITY-ERLEBNISSE BIETEN DERZEIT GROSSES POTENZIAL.

Mit der Technologie kann Unsichtbares mittlerweile auf realistische Art und Weise sichtbar gemacht werden und so für Begeisterung sorgen. Selbst die Vermittlung spezieller Fachinhalte, zum Beispiel die Funktionsweise von einem Antriebsstrang, kann so zu einem echten Erlebnis werden. Dabei spielen gelungenes Storytelling und ein gutes Sounddesign eine oft unterschätzte Rolle.

Sören Fricke: Die Möglichkeiten des Layerings von Inhalten sind ein spannendes und recht neues Feld. Ob es dabei nun unter dem Schlagwort AR oder XR/MR geführt wird, ist im Grunde egal. Wie bereits weiter oben erwähnt, die Technologie ist ohnehin nicht der Zweck an sich – sie ist der Hammer, um den Nagel zu versenken, also die Botschaft zu überbringen. VR ist aus meiner Sicht eine End-of-Life-Technologie.

Sustainability is just as big a topic. Technologies can help to develop long-term solutions. At the same time, they use a lot of resources – especially the currently popular AIs. How do you handle this problem?

Sören Fricke: The experience sector with exhibitions, events and a focus on the moment is of course faced with a big challenge when it comes to sustainability, especially in the ecological sense of the word. Projects should be viewed especially in terms of their lifecycle. Does something have to be created just for this one moment or can it also serve more than one moment? Are there perhaps other ways of achieving the required aim that use up fewer resources? Can the aim itself be adjusted in order to develop something more long-term or less resource-intensive?

Christoph Diederichs: Our experience shows that interactive experiences have quite a long half-life period. This should be taken into account when setting aims, when developing the concept and also in the realisation. The application should then not be used just at a single event but be used continuously over several years – as we know, software can easily be developed further and updated.

A glimpse into the future: What current projects, research projects or experimental technologies are you observing with particular interest?

Christoph Diederichs: We are still waiting for marketable AR glasses that are affordable for end customers and weigh less than 300 grams. Holograms or 3D displays that don't require glasses are also particularly interesting. In the field of VR, a lot is happening with the Bigscreen Beyond 2 – especially when it comes to minimisation and weight reduction. In addition, we are always keen to observe conferences such as SIGGRAPH, where interesting papers or products are presented.

Sören Fricke: Basically, there is nothing that clearly stands out for us at the moment. Perhaps the increasingly more comprehensively available transparent video surfaces are worth a mention, whether as LED or OLED. The possibilities opened by viewing what is "behind", with the possibility of communication on the transparent layer in front, have definitely not yet been fully exploited.

Technological possibilities are developing at a fast pace – from VR, AR and MR to interactive tracking systems and artificial intelligence. In your view, what developments or technologies currently have the greatest influence on experience design? And why?

Christoph Diederichs:

AUGMENTED REALITY EXPERIENCES CURRENTLY OFFER GREAT POTENTIAL.

The technology now allows the invisible to be made visible in a realistic manner, sparking enthusiasm. Even conveying special professional content, such as how a drive train functions, can be turned into a real experience. Successful storytelling and a good sound design often play an underestimated role.

Sören Fricke: The possibilities of layering content are an interesting and rather new field. Whether it comes under the byword AR or XR/MR basically doesn't matter. As already mentioned further above, technology is in any case not an end in itself – it is the hammer with which to hit the nail, to convey the message. In my view, VR is an end-of-life technology.

Während der Pandemie wurde virtuellen Erlebnissen – insbesondere dem Metaverse – eine große Zukunft vorausgesagt. Diese Vision hat sich bislang nicht durchgesetzt. Woran liegt das?

Christoph Diederichs: Wir haben den Metaverse-Hype nie besonders ernst genommen. Wir als Menschen wollen doch menschliche Erlebnisse haben und dazu gehört eben auch die physische Erfahrung. Außerdem waren die ersten Ansätze der Metaverse ja nichts Neues. Jedes Online-Computerspiel ist mehr oder weniger eine Art Metaverse, das hat besipielsweise World of Warcraft schon Jahre zuvor unter Beweis gestellt.

Sören Fricke: Virtuelle Erlebnisse sprechen im Normalfall maximal zwei Sinne an: das Visuelle und das Auditive. Live-Erlebnisse im Raum sprechen dabei aber viel mehr Sinne an, daher sind die Erlebnisse intensiver und damit nachhaltiger.

DER VIRTUELLE RAUM IST HERVORRAGEND FÜR DIE KOMMUNIKATION INHALTLICHER ZUSAMMENHÄNGE, SCHAFFT ABER NUR SCHWER EINE EMOTIONALE TIEFE.

Live ist die emotionale Tiefe sehr leicht zu erreichen, der Inhalt aber trotzdem ausreichend gut zu kommunizieren.

Was hat sich stattdessen aus den Erfahrungen dieser Zeit entwickelt und etabliert?

Christoph Diederichs: QR-Codes sind endlich im Mainstream angekommen! – Spaß beiseite, für uns war es hauptsächlich die Bestätigung und Sicherheit darüber, dass physische Erlebnisse einfach unverzichtbar sind. Gerade im Bereich der Kulturprojekte wurde deutlich, wie sehr Menschen den direkten, sinnlichen Zugang zu Inhalten schätzen – ob durch Ausstellungen, Installationen oder interaktive Formate vor Ort. Digitale Elemente können diese Erlebnisse sinnvoll ergänzen, aber definitiv nicht ersetzen.

Sören Fricke: Noch nicht vollständig etabliert, liegt die Zukunft aber im ganzheitlichen, individuellen Erlebnis. Die virtuelle und die physische Welt müssen verschmelzen und jede von ihnen ihre Vorteile voll ausspielen.

Für die Nutzenden darf es sich dabei nicht anfühlen, als wären es getrennte Welten. Die Erlebnisse und Inhalte aus dem Virtuellen müssen live eine Ergänzung erfahren und sich dann wieder ins Virtuell-Digitale weiterspannen. Es geht um die individuelle, persönliche Erfahrung, die „nur für mich" gemacht ist. Mit neuen Werkzeugen wie Big Data, LLMs und genAI, gepaart mit einer komplett neuen Denkweise der User Experience, ergeben sich daraus Erlebnisse, die wirklich nachhaltig inspirieren und länger als den einen Moment andauern.

Vielen Dank für die wertvollen und aufschlussreichen Einblicke!

During the pandemic, it was predicted that virtual experiences – especially metaverse – would have a great future. This vision has not yet come to fruition. Why is that?

Christoph Diederichs: We never took the metaverse hype very seriously. We as people want to have human experiences, after all, and this includes physical experiences. Furthermore, the initial metaverse approaches were nothing new. Every online computer game is more or less a kind of metaverse, as proven for example by World of Warcraft years ago.

Sören Fricke: Virtual experiences normally appeal to a maximum of two senses: the visual and the auditory. Live spatial experiences, on the other hand, appeal to a lot more senses, therefore the experiences are more intense and memorable.

VIRTUAL SPACE IS EXCELLENT FOR COMMUNICATING CONTENTUAL CONTEXTS BUT STRUGGLES TO CREATE EMOTIONAL DEPTH.

It is very easy to achieve emotional depth live, while at the same time adequately communicating the content.

What has developed and established itself instead since then out of the experiences during this time?

Christoph Diederichs: QR codes have finally become mainstream! – But kidding aside, for us it was mainly the confirmation and certainty that physical experiences are simply essential. It became clear especially in the field of cultural projects how much people appreciate direct, meaningful access to content – whether through exhibitions, installations or interactive formats on site. Digital elements can meaningfully supplement these experiences but definitely not replace them.

Sören Fricke: It's not yet fully established, but the future lies in immersive, individual experiences. The virtual and physical world must blend and each of them must display their advantages to the full.

However, for the users it must not feel as if they are separate worlds. The experiences and content that are virtual must be supplemented live and then extend further into the virtual and digital. It is about the individual, personal experience made "just for me". With new tools such as Big Data, LLMs and genAI, coupled with a completely new way of thinking regarding the user experience, experiences result that leave a truly inspiring impression and last more than just the one moment.

Thank you so much for these valuable and informative insights!

Jede Zielgruppe hat unterschiedliche Bedürfnisse und Erwartungen. Dementsprechend sind Eventkonzepte im Idealfall nicht nur auf den Absender, sondern vor allem auf die Empfänger zugeschnitten.

PUBLIC: EINE BREITE ÖFFENTLICHKEIT, DIE SICH AUS EINWOHNERN, TOURISTEN, PASSANTEN, FLANEUREN ETC. ZUFÄLLIG ZUSAMMENSETZT. DEMENTSPRECHEND HETEROGEN – IN (SOZIALER) HERKUNFT, ALTER ODER VORLIEBEN – ZEIGT SICH DIESE ZIELGRUPPE, DIE NICHT NUR SEHR GROSS, SONDERN IN DER ANSPRACHE NICHT EINDEUTIG ZU FASSEN IST. WAS DEN JEWEILIGEN PERSONEN ALLERDINGS GEMEIN IST, IST EIN NICHT KOMMERZIELLES INTERESSE.

PUBLIC

Each target group has different requirements and expectations. Event concepts are therefore ideally not only geared towards the addressor, but especially towards the recipients.

PUBLIC: A WIDER PUBLIC IS COMPOSED BY CHANCE OF INHABITANTS, TOURISTS, PASSERS-BY ETC. THIS TARGET GROUP IS HETEROGENEOUS ACCORDINGLY – IN TERMS OF (SOCIAL) BACKGROUND, AGE OR PREFERENCES – AND IS NOT ONLY VERY LARGE, BUT ALSO DIFFICULT TO GRASP IN TERMS OF APPEAL. HOWEVER, WHAT THESE PEOPLE HAVE IN COMMON IS A NON-COMMERCIAL INTEREST.

PUBLIC

ZEYREK ÇINILI HAMAM

ATELIER BRÜCKNER, STUTTGART

Location
Çavuşdere Cad Çinili Hamam Sok No 6, Istanbul

Client
Marmara Group Dış Tic.Ltd.Şti., Istanbul

Month / Year
September 2023 (Opening)

Duration
Permanent

Awards
Silver (Spatial Experience – Exhibition – Exhibition for Subject – Exhibition) at ADC Awards 2024; Silver (Space – Experimental) at CommAwards 2024; Architecture Masterprize 2024 (Exhibition)

Direction / Coordination
ATELIER BRÜCKNER, Stuttgart

Architecture / Design
ATELIER BRÜCKNER, Stuttgart (Exhibition design); KA-BA, Ankara (Architecture, Expansion and conversion)

Lighting
Belzner Holmes Light-Design, Stuttgart

Media
medienprojekt p2, Stuttgart

Music
Youmna Saba, Beirut

Others
amplify design, Stuttgart; H5, Paris; Bunni Studio, London (Media projection); DS Architecture (Landscape architecture)

Photos
Giovanni Emilio Galanello, Milan

Zeyrek Cinili Hamam, a 16th-century masterpiece by the architect Sinan, has been turned into a hybrid venue comprising a bathhouse, museum and event space over the course of a twelve-year renovation. The scenography and exhibition by ATELIER BRÜCKNER preserve the historical substance and at the same time create a modern world of experience where tradition and innovation merge.

Der Zeyrek Çinili Hamam, ein Meisterwerk des Architekten Sinan aus dem 16. Jahrhundert, wurde nach einer zwölfjährigen Restaurierung zu einem hybriden Ort aus Badehaus, Museum und Veranstaltungsraum. Die Szenografie und Ausstellung von ATELIER BRÜCKNER bewahrt die historische Substanz und schafft zugleich eine moderne Erlebniswelt, in der Tradition und Innovation verschmelzen.

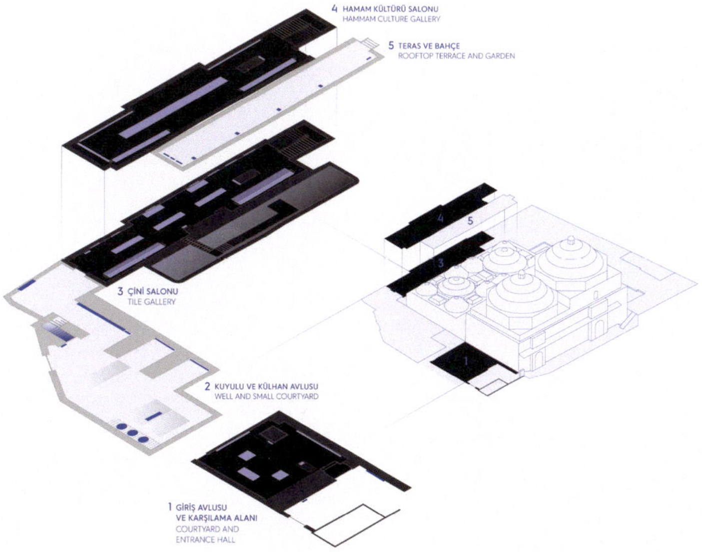

Die Ausstellung gliedert sich in vier thematische Bereiche, die die Geschichte und Kultur des Hamams erlebbar machen. Im Foyer gibt „The Story of Hamam" mit historischen Einblicken in Architektur und Restaurierung eine Einführung. Der Innenhof inszeniert mit der Lichtskulptur „Journey of Water, Smoke and Steam" die historische Wasserversorgung des Hamams. In der „Tiles Gallery" entfalten interaktive Medien die Schönheit der İznik-Fliesenfragmente, während die „Bathing Culture Gallery" mit einer Sammlung von 70 traditionellen Bade-Clogs das rituelle Erbe der Hamam-Kultur beleuchtet.

The exhibition is divided into four themed areas that show the history and culture of the hamam. "The Story of Hamam" in the foyer with historical insights into the architecture and restoration provides an introduction. The interior courtyard stages the historical water supply to the hamam with the light sculpture "Journey of Water, Smoke and Steam". In the "Tiles Gallery", interactive media highlight the beauty of the İznik tile fragments, while the "Bathing Culture Gallery" illuminates the ritual heritage of hammam culture with a collection of 70 traditional bathing clogs.

Die Szenografie verbindet traditionelle Materialien mit modernen Elementen. Dunkelgrauer Stahl, Cortenstahl und Marmara-Marmor betonen die historische Architektur. Durch gezieltes Lichtdesign entstehen eindrucksvolle Akzente, die Wasserbewegungen nachempfinden. Klanglandschaften von Youmna Saba verstärken die immersive Atmosphäre.

The scenography combines traditional materials with modern elements. Dark grey steel, corten steel and Marmara marble emphasise the historical architecture. A targeted lighting design creates impressive accents that mimic the movements of water. The immersive atmosphere is enhanced by sound landscapes by Youmna Saba.

EIN KULTURELLES JUWEL ALS ZEITGEMÄSSE ERLEBNISWELT, DIE TRADITION UND INNOVATION HARMONISCH VEREINT.

Neben der einzigartigen Kombination aus funktionierendem Hamam, Ausstellung und Eventraum vereint das Projekt eine harmonische Balance aus historischer Authentizität und innovativen Technologien. Interaktive Medieninstallationen rekonstruieren das ursprüngliche Fliesendekor, während die Markenidentität, die in Zusammenarbeit mit H5 Paris entwickelt wurde, mit Schriften und Grafikelementen die visuelle Sprache des Ortes prägt. Eine interaktive App und begleitende Website erweitern das Erlebnis in den digitalen Raum.

Alongside the unique combination of a functioning hamam, an exhibition and an event space, the project brings together a harmonious balance of historical authenticity and innovative technologies. Interactive media installations reconstruct the original tile décor, while the visual language of the venue features the brand identity, which was developed in cooperation with H5 Paris, with inscriptions and graphic elements. An interactive app and accompanying website extend the experience into digital space.

A CULTURAL JEWEL AS A CONTEMPORARY WORLD OF EXPERIENCE WHICH HARMONIOUSLY BRINGS TOGETHER TRADITION AND INNOVATION.

PETRONAS
SONAX
FINISH

"BOXENSTOPP" @MYTHOSRAUM 7 OF THE MERCEDES-BENZ MUSEUM – AN INTERACTIVE FORMULA 1 EXPERIENCE

ATELIER MARKGRAPH GMBH, FRANKFURT AM MAIN

Location
Mercedes-Benz Museum, Stuttgart

Client
Mercedes-Benz Heritage GmbH, Stuttgart

Month / Year
January 2025 (Completion)

Duration
Permanent

Concept / Staging / Design / Realisation
Atelier Markgraph GmbH, Frankfurt am Main

Overall artistic direction
merz merz GmbH & Co. KG, Berlin

Graphic production
Eicher Werkstätten GmbH & Co. KG, Kernen im Remstal

Construction
Raumtechnik Messebau & Event Services GmbH, Ostfildern

Others
Expotec Pro GmbH, Mainz (Exhibit construction); Atelier Markgraph GmbH, Frankfurt am Main (Software)

Photos
Kai Loges | die arge lola, Stuttgart

Die neue Boxenstopp-Experience im Mythosraum 7 des Mercedes-Benz Museums macht den Mythos Formel 1 interaktiv erlebbar. Im Mittelpunkt stehen nicht nur Geschwindigkeit und Rekorde, sondern die entscheidenden Faktoren des Motorsports: Teamwork, Strategie und Präzision. Das von Atelier Markgraph gestaltete Erlebnis lässt Besucherinnen und Besucher Teil eines Rennteams werden und aktiv in die Welt hinter den Kulissen eintauchen.

AN INTERACTIVE STAGING OF DECISIVE FACTORS IN MOTORSPORTS: TEAMWORK, STRATEGY AND PRECISION.

The new Boxenstopp (pit stop) in Myth Room 7 of the Mercedes-Benz Museum provides an interactive experience of the Formula 1 myth. The focus is not only on speed and records but also on the factors that are decisive in motorsports: teamwork, strategy and precision. The experience designed by Atelier Markgraph allows visitors to become part of a racing team and to immerse themselves actively in the world behind the scenes.

Schon beim Betreten der Erlebniszone spüren die Teilnehmenden die Atmosphäre eines Boxenstopps. In einem detailgetreu gestalteten Setting übernehmen sie zentrale Rollen – an der Pit Wall, bei der Radwechselstation oder im Strategiebereich. Jede Aufgabe erfordert Schnelligkeit, Reaktionsvermögen und kluge Entscheidungen. Nur mit taktischem Geschick und echtem Teamgeist lassen sich die besten Zeiten und Highscores erreichen.

ENTSCHEIDENDE FAKTOREN DES MOTORSPORTS INTERAKTIV INSZENIERT: TEAMWORK, STRATEGIE UND PRÄZISION.

As soon as they enter the experience zone, participants can feel the atmosphere of a pit stop. They take on central roles in the setting with a realistically detailed design – at the pit wall, at the wheel changing station or in the strategy area. Each task requires speed, quick responses and clever decisions. It is only with tactical skills and a true team spirit that the best times and high scores can be achieved.

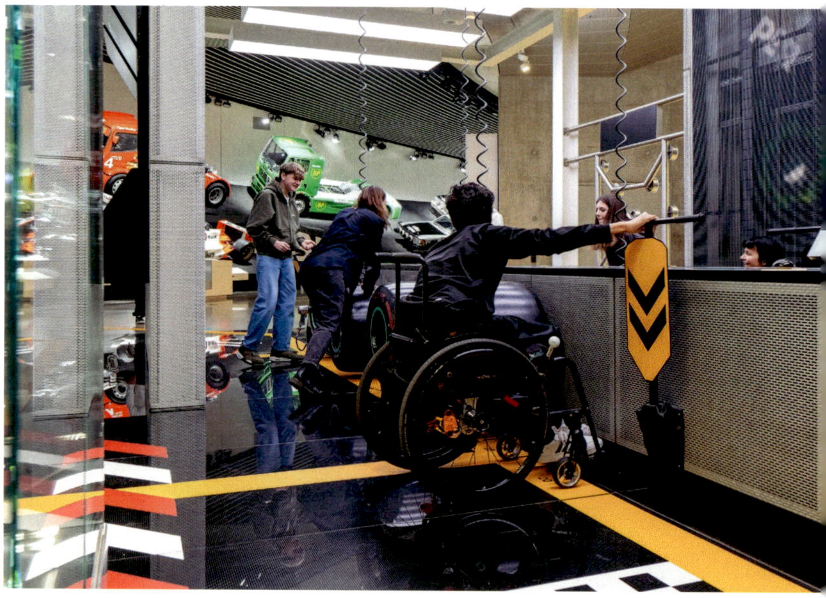

Dynamische Lichtinszenierungen, realistische Sounds und interaktive Displays verstärken die immersive Wirkung. Realität und Simulation verschmelzen – das Adrenalin steigt, die Spannung wird greifbar. Hinter dem Spielspaß verbirgt sich auch eine tiefere Mission: Die Experience setzt auf zukunftsweisende Edutainment-Elemente, die Wissen über den Motorsport spielerisch vermitteln und zugleich digitale Daten für die Evaluation generieren.

Dynamic plays of light, realistic sounds and interactive displays enhance the immersive effect. Reality and simulation merge – adrenaline mounts, the tension becomes palpable. There is a deeper mission behind the playful fun: The experience makes use of pioneering edutainment elements that convey knowledge about motorsports in a playful manner and at the same time generate digital data for evaluation.

Der neue Erlebnisbereich richtet sich gezielt an eine junge, digital affine Zielgruppe, spricht aber auch traditionelle Motorsportfans an. Die Verbindung aus praktischer Erfahrung und Wissensvermittlung macht den Boxenstopp zu einem integrativen Bestandteil des Museums – ein interaktives Highlight für alle, die den Motorsport aus einer neuen Perspektive erleben wollen.

The new experience area is aimed at a young, digitally savvy visitor target group, while also appealing to traditional motorsports fans. The combination of practical experience and conveying knowledge makes the pit stop an integral part of the museum – an interactive highlight for all those who would like to experience motorsports from a new perspective.

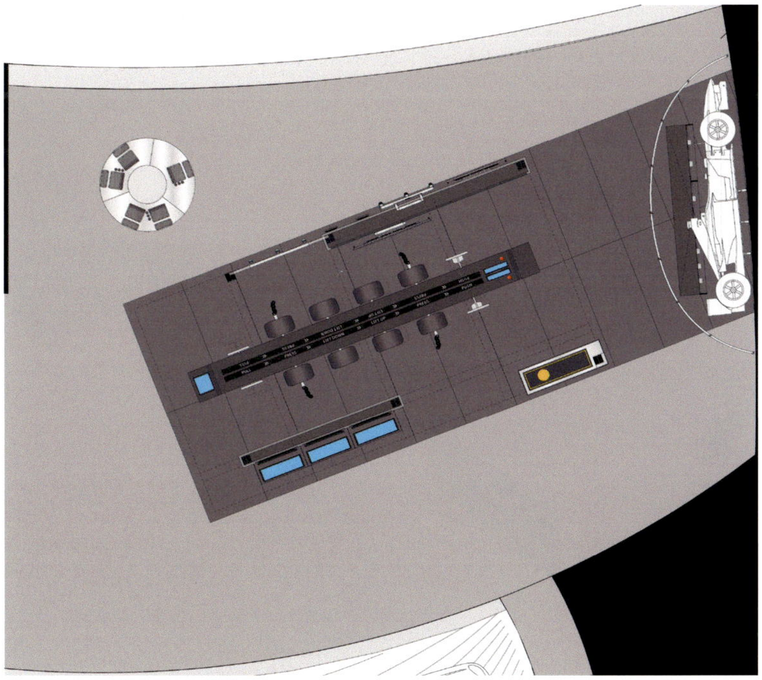

MOVE
kostenlose
Austellung

PUBLIC

MOVE – HOME OF THE MARATHON

DIE WELLENMASCHINE GMBH, BERLIN

Location
Platz des 18. März, Brandenburger Tor, Berlin

Client
SSC Event GmbH, Berlin

Month / Year
September 2024

Duration
15 days

Dramaturgy / Direction / Coordination / Media
die wellenmaschine GmbH, Berlin

Architecture / Design / Decoration
studio bonn.berlin, Berlin

Graphics
studio bonn.berlin, Berlin; Studio Riethmüller, Berlin

Lighting
Krsn Brasko, Berlin

Films
die wellenmaschine GmbH, Berlin; Uetz Kaimira, Berlin; Rebellab Fimproduktion, Berlin

Music
Poetry Meets; Roseneck Boys; Marcus Klossek Trio; Tuba Vibes Project; Andrea Marcelli Quartett and others

Artists / Show acts
Friedrich Liechtenstein; Hajo Schumacher and others

Catering
Max Frey, Berlin

Construction
kpm3 AG, Diessenhofen

Others
Claudius Brodmann, Berlin (Exhibition curation)

Photos
die wellenmaschine GmbH, Berlin

The first Berlin people's marathon was held in 1974 in the Grunewald region with 274 runners. Today it is among the largest running events in the world. In 2024 the BMW BERLIN MARATHON celebrated its 50th anniversary – with over 50,000 participants.

The agency die wellenmaschine was appointed at an early stage by SCC Events, the organiser of the BERLIN MARATHON, to realise a special idea: a house at Brandenburg Gate, as a thank you to the city and its people and a place that tells the history of the BERLIN MARATHON. It is not only about sport, it is interwoven with the city of Berlin itself – and therefore also with world history. The result was MOVE: a temporary building that blends architecturally with its surroundings. It is open, inviting and on two levels – crowned by a light sculpture and golden flags.

1974 startete im Grunewald der erste Berliner Volksmarathon mit 274 Läufer:innen. Heute gehört er zu einer der größten Laufveranstaltungen der Welt. 2024 feierte der BMW BERLIN-MARATHON sein 50-jähriges Bestehen – mit über 50.000 Teilnehmenden.

Im Vorfeld wurde die wellenmaschine von der SCC Events, Veranstalterin des BERLIN-MARATHON, mit der Umsetzung einer besonderen Idee betraut: Ein Haus am Brandenburger Tor. Ein Dank an die Stadt und ihre Menschen. Ein Ort, der die Geschichte des BERLIN-MARATHON erzählt. Diese umfasst nicht nur den Sport, sondern ist mit der Stadt Berlin selbst verwoben – und damit auch mit der Weltgeschichte. Enstanden ist der MOVE: ein temporärer Bau, der sich architektonisch in seine Umgebung einfügt. Offen, einladend, auf zwei Ebenen – gekrönt von einer Lichtskulptur und goldenen Fahnen.

EIN TEMPORÄRER ERLEBNISRAUM ALS DANK AN DIE STADT UND IHRE MENSCHEN.

Das Programm, das die Gäste im offenen Patio erlebten, teilte sich in 50 Veranstaltungen in 15 Tagen. Darunter interaktive Formate wie Lauftreffs, Yoga und Workouts für alle Altersgruppen nebst fachlichen Panels zu Marathon- und Sportthemen – für Stadtgesellschaft und Läufer:innen, egal ob Profi oder Amateur. Highlights des Entertainmentprogramms waren Formate wie Poetry meets MOVE, Jazzbands von der Strecke oder Lesungen aus Laufliteratur.

Die Ausstellung im Obergeschoss ließ die Geschichte des Events Revue passieren: 50 Jahre BERLIN-MARATHON auf 200 Quadratmetern, widergespiegelt in Pokalen, Urkunden, Schuhen, Medaillen, Fotos der kleinen und großen Momente sowie persönlichen Interviews von Zeug:innen und Macher:innen. So entstand aus vielen kleinen Geschichten eine große Erzählung.

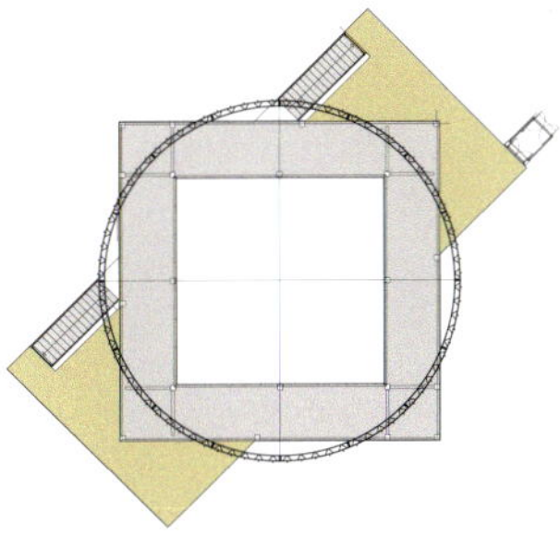

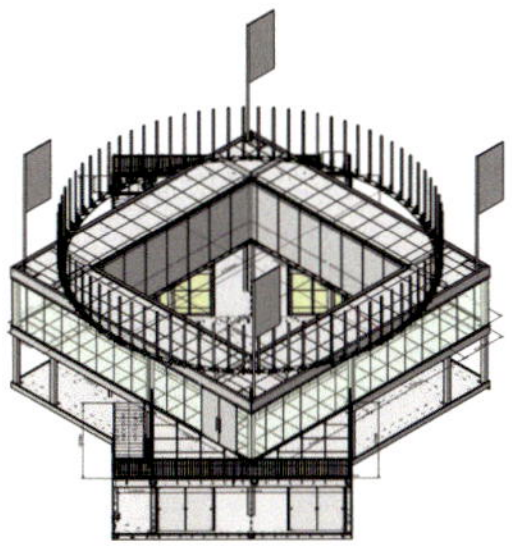

The programme that guests experienced on the open patio was spread over 50 events on 15 days. It offered interactive formats such as running meets, yoga and workouts for all age groups, alongside specialist panels on marathon and sport topics – for the urban population and the runners, whether professional or amateur. The highlights of the entertainment programme included formats such as Poetry meets MOVE, jazz bands or readings from running literature.

A TEMPORARY SPATIAL EXPERIENCE AS A THANK YOU TO THE CITY AND ITS PEOPLE.

The exhibition on the upper floor recounted the history of the event: 50 years of BERLIN MARATHON on 200 square metres, reflected in trophies, certificates, shoes, medals, photos of the small and big moments, as well as personal interviews with witnesses and participants. This turned many little stories into a big narrative.

PUBLIC

UTOPIAN GARDEN

FLORA&FAUNAVISIONS GMBH, BERLIN

Location
Various (Touring)

IP Owner / Concept / Design / Production
flora&faunavisions GmbH, Berlin

Month / Year
May 2023 (Premiere)

Duration
Ongoing

Awards
Gold (Best Thematic Exhibition) at BrandEx 2025; WXO Experience Awards 2024 (Science)

Soundtrack
Julian Ganzer / Ilja Coric, Berlin

Sound design
Julian Ganzer / Studio Kreuzberg, Berlin

Music games art / Science / Nature
Asako Fujimoto, Berlin

Interactive programming
wirmachenbunt GmbH & Co. KG, Hamburg

Photos
flora&faunavisions Lacey Wright, Berlin

Utopian Garden ist ein von flora&faunavisions gestaltetes immersives Erlebnis, das die Schönheit der Natur, der Kunst und des menschlichen Potenzials zelebriert. Besucherinnen und Besucher werden ermutigt, die Verbindungen zwischen Wissenschaft, Natur und Kunst, ihr Potenzial und die Wunder der Welt interaktiv zu entdecken.

Utopian Garden is an immersive experience designed by flora&faunavisions that celebrates the beauty of nature, art and human potential. Visitors are encouraged to interactively explore connections between science, nature and art, as well as their potential and the wonders of the world.

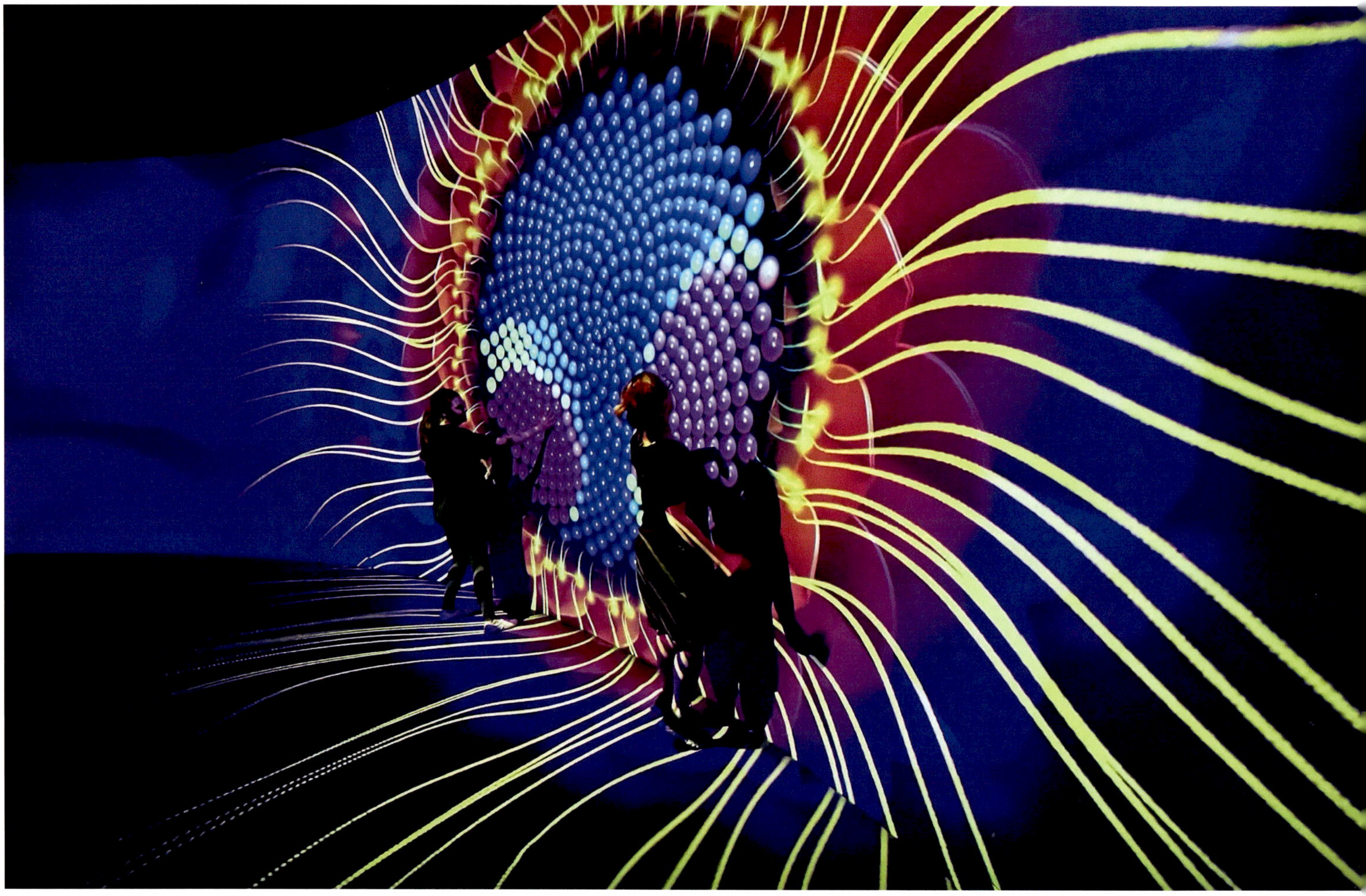

EIN IMMERSIVES ERLEBNIS MACHT DIE VERBINDUNG VON WISSENSCHAFT, NATUR UND KUNST KOLLEKTIV ERFAHRBAR.

AN IMMERSIVE EXPERIENCE PROVIDES A COLLECTIVE EXPE-RIENCE OF THE FUSION OF SCIENCE, NATURE AND ART.

Das 45-minütige Erlebnis ist in drei Kapitel gegliedert – Wissenschaft, Natur und Kunst. Eingerahmt von einer 15-minütigen Pre-Show und einem 30-minütigen Post-Show-Workshop, lässt es die Besucher:innen voll und ganz in das Geschehen eintauchen. Sie werden durch eine digitale Landschaft geführt und interagieren mit visuellen Szenen, um ihre eigenen Erfahrungen zu gestalten und damit zu einer kollektiven utopischen Vision beizutragen. Das abschließende Highlight ist die Enthüllung des „Utopischen Gartens" – einer gemeinsamen Schöpfung, die Hoffnung, Kreativität und Co-Creation symbolisiert.

The 45-minute experience is divided into three chapters – science, nature and art. It enables visitors to immerse themselves fully in the goings on, within the framework of a 15-minute pre-show and a 30-minute post-show workshop. They are guided through a digital landscape and interact with visual scenes, in order to create their own experiences and to thereby contribute to a collective utopian vision. The concluding highlight is the revelation of a "Utopian Garden" – a joint creation that symbolises hope, creativity and co-creation.

Im Anschluss an die Show können die Gäste in praktisch gelagerten Workshops selbst aktiv werden – und Blattabdrücke, Samenbomben oder nachhaltige Anstecknadeln gestalten. Der Austausch mit anderen Teilnehmenden verstärkt das Gemeinschaftsgefühl und unterstreicht dadurch das Leitbild des Projekts.

Die multimediale Inszenierung vereint modernste Technologien mit emotionalem Storytelling. Sie wurde für bis zu 120 Gäste pro Vorstellung entwickelt und bietet eine flexible, global einsetzbare Infrastruktur, die eine Fernsteuerung aus Deutschland ermöglicht. Seit der Weltpremiere in Seattle/Tacoma im Mai 2023 ist Utopian Garden auf internationaler Tournee.

Following on from the show, guests have the opportunity to join in actively themselves in practical workshops, creating paper prints, seed bombs or sustainable badges. Interaction with other participants strengthens the community feeling and reinforces the project's mission.

The multimedia staging combines an array of the latest technologies with emotional storytelling. It was developed for up to 120 guests per performance and offers a flexible, universally usable infrastructure that allows remote control from Germany. Utopian Garden has been touring internationally since its world premiere in Seattle/Tacoma in May 2023.

Hotel HEIMAT
Multimediale
Ausstellung
2023
57

PUBLIC

HOTEL HEIMAT – A MULTIMEDIA EXPERIENCE

KOLLEKTIV URBANPROJECTION, LÜBECK

Location
Hotel zur alten Stadtmauer, Lübeck

Concept
Kollektiv UrbanProjection, Lübeck; Various foundations and non-profit organisations (Funding)

Month / Year
November 2023 (Premiere: March 2023)

Duration
4 days

Dramaturgy / Direction / Coordination / Design / Graphics / Lighting / Media / Films / Decoration
UrbanProjection – Kollektiv für urbane Erzählformate (Andrea Bohacz; Barbara Duraj; Christoffer Greiß; Mathias Hollaender) in cooperation with Peter Grünig and Franziska Grünig-Volp

Photos
Andrea Bohacz; Christoffer Greiß; Mathias Hollaender

EINE AUDIOVISUELLE AUSSTELLUNG ERZÄHLT BERÜHREND VON FLUCHT, VERTREIBUNG UND NEUBEGINN.

Im März und November 2023 öffnete das Lübecker „Hotel zur alten Stadtmauer" mehrere Tage seine Türen für rund 2.500 Besucher:innen. Voll belegt und in den laufenden Hotelbetrieb integriert, präsentierte es eine einzigartige multimediale Installation: Hotel Heimat, eine audiovisuelle Ausstellung, die sich mit Flucht, Vertreibung und Neubeginn auseinandersetzte.

Im Hotel werden Menschen, die ihre Heimat verlassen haben, mit offenen Armen empfangen. Hier finden sie Freundschaft und Unterstützung für einen Neubeginn. Der perfekte Ort für eine multisensorische Reise in persönliche Geschichten und Schicksale.

Das Projekt des Kollektivs UrbanProjection lässt Betroffene in 16 Stationen von berührenden Themen wie Flucht, Vertreibung und Neubeginn erzählen. Die Installationen sind teils raumgreifend, bewegt und dynamisch, teils versteckt, klein und geheimnisvoll – und ins gesamte Hotel eingebettet: Sie finden sich in den Zimmern, den Fluren, der Küche oder im Waschraum.

In March and November 2023, the "Hotel zur alten Stadtmauer" in Lübeck opened its doors for several days to around 2500 visitors. It was fully booked and integrated into the ongoing running of the hotel, presenting a unique multimedia installation: Hotel Heimat (Homeland Hotel), which addressed the issues of fleeing, displacement and new beginnings.

People who had left their homeland were welcomed with open arms at the hotel, where they could find friendship and support in order to start afresh. It was the perfect place for a multisensory journey into personal stories and fates.

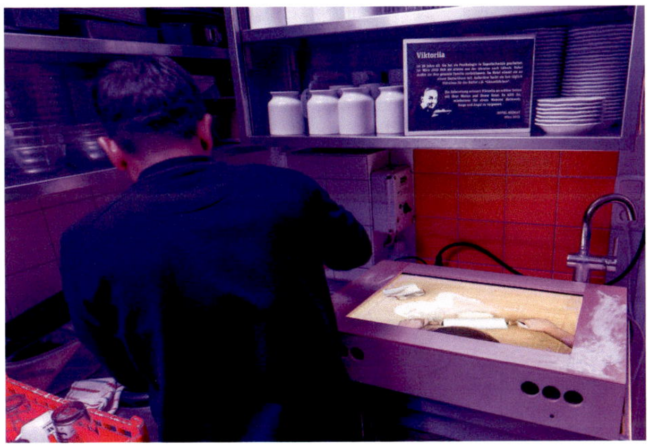

The project by the collective UrbanProjection allowed those affected to tell moving stories about fleeing, displacement and new beginnings at 16 stations. Some of the installations were extensive, animated and dynamic, while others were hidden, small and mysterious – and distributed around the entirety of the hotel, in rooms, corridors, the kitchen or the washroom.

On their circuit, visitors discovered objects such as a white table with hands that drew a map and explain fleeing routes, while a bowl with nuts wandered back and forth on the table. In one of the rooms, they faced a young man called Rami who recounted his father's dream of building a house, the nightmare of losing it again in the war and his own dream of rebuilding this house somewhere else in a different country. Guests lifted the lid of a pot in the kitchen. On the floor they could see a dish, a maqluba, being cooked – by Mohammad, whose mother in Syria was giving him instructions by telephone. Everyone was brought together at an international buffet, where the protagonists, the hotel team and the visitors met and interacted.

Besuchende entdeckten beim Rundgang unter anderem einen weißen Tisch mit Händen, die eine Landkarte zeichnen und Fluchtrouten erklären, während eine Schale mit Nüssen auf dem Tisch hin und her wandert. In einem Zimmer lagen sie einem jungen Mann, Rami, gegenüber. Er erzählt vom Traum seines Vaters, ein Haus zu bauen, vom Alptraum, es im Krieg wieder zu verlieren, und von seinem eigenen Traum, dieses Haus wieder zu bauen, an einem anderen Ort in einem anderen Land. In der Küche hoben Gäste den Deckel eines Topfes an. Auf dem Boden sahen sie, wie ein Gericht, eine Maklube, gekocht wird – von Mohammad, dessen Mutter in Syrien ihm telefonisch die Anweisungen gibt. Ein internationales Büfett, an dem sich die Protagonist:innen, das Hotelteam und Besucher:innen zum Austausch trafen, verband alle und schuf Begegnungsmomente.

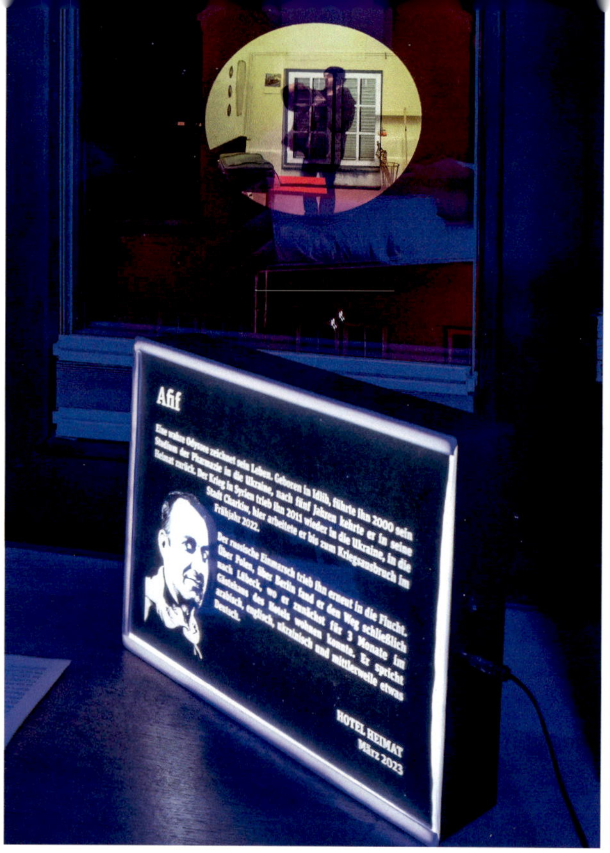

AN AUDIOVISUAL EXHIBITION TELLS THE MOVING STORY OF FLEEING, DISPLACEMENT AND NEW BEGINNINGS.

The concept set out to include the participating persons, to reflect together on the topics of refugees and homeland and to develop creative transformation strategies. This resulted in an artistic format that people can identify with and that authentically describes their situation. At the same time, the sharing of these sensitive topics helped the processing of individual experiences and enriched the collective team with insights into previously unknown worlds and lives.

Bei der Konzeption wurden die handelnden Personen bewusst eingebunden, das Thema Flucht und Heimat gemeinsam reflektiert und kreative Transformationsstrategien entwickelt. Auf diese Art fand sich eine künstlerische Form, in der sich die Menschen wiedererkennen und die ihre Situation authentisch beschreibt. Zugleich trug der sensible Austausch zum Verarbeitungsprozess der individuellen Erfahrungen bei und bereicherte das Team des Kollektivs mit Einblicken in bislang unbekannte Lebenswelten.

Nach Abschluss der Hotelausstellung werden die einzelnen Installationen zu verschiedenen Anlässen auch an anderen Orten gezeigt, wie zum Beispiel im Rahmen des Thementags FLUCHT im Industriemuseum Geschichtswerkstatt Herrenwyk oder bei den Offenen Ateliers im VersuchsHaus Lübeck.

After the end of the hotel exhibition, the individual installations were also shown at other venues on various occasions, such as during the theme day FLEEING at the Industriemuseum Geschichtswerkstatt Herrenwyk (Herrenwyk Industrial Museum and History Workshop) or at the Open Ateliers at VersuchsHaus Lübeck.

Mitmachen
11
10
9

PUBLIC

FLOCK OF

BIT.STUDIO, BANGKOK

Location
Ars Electronica Festival 2024, Post City, Linz

Client
Ars Electronica Festival 2024, Linz

Month / Year
September 2024

Duration
5 days

Direction / Design / Technology / Robotics
bit.studio, Bangkok

Photos
bit.studio, Bangkok

EIN SPIEL AUS KUNST, TECHNOLOGIE UND WISSENSCHAFT SOLL DIE VERFLECHTUNG DER WELT SICHTBAR MACHEN.

FLOCK OF questions our perceptions and invites us to explore the boundaries between fantasy and reality anew. The artistic installation by bit.studio from Thailand entices the public into a world where shapes dissolve and are recomposed. A shoal of floating fish emerges in a surreal metamorphosis – an interplay of light, movement and structure that shows the interrelation of the world.

As the drifting creatures move through the space, they undergo a subtle but profound transformation. Similar to a flock of birds that changes direction in unison, they collectively take on a new identity and reflect the constant flux of being.

This vision comes alive through the combination of science, technology and art. FLOCK OF makes use of a precise choreography of physics, mechanics and digital controls to create an immersive experience. Every balloon filled with helium is fitted with a special control chip that records its position in the air and coordinates its movements – a harmonious interplay of algorithms and aesthetic dynamics.

FLOCK OF hinterfragt unsere Wahrnehmung und lädt dazu ein, die Grenzen zwischen Fantasie und Realität neu zu erkunden. Die künstlerische Installation des thailändischen bit.studio entführt das Publikum in eine Welt, in der Formen sich auflösen und neu zusammensetzen. Ein Schwarm schwebender Fische entfaltet sich in einer surrealen Metamorphose – ein Spiel aus Licht, Bewegung und Struktur, das die Verflechtung der natürlichen Welt sichtbar macht.

Während sich die schwebenden Wesen durch den Raum bewegen, durchlaufen sie eine subtile, aber tiefgreifende Transformation. Ähnlich wie ein Vogelschwarm, der seine Richtung im Gleichklang ändert, nimmt dieses Kollektiv eine neue Identität an und spiegelt die ständige Veränderung des Daseins wider.

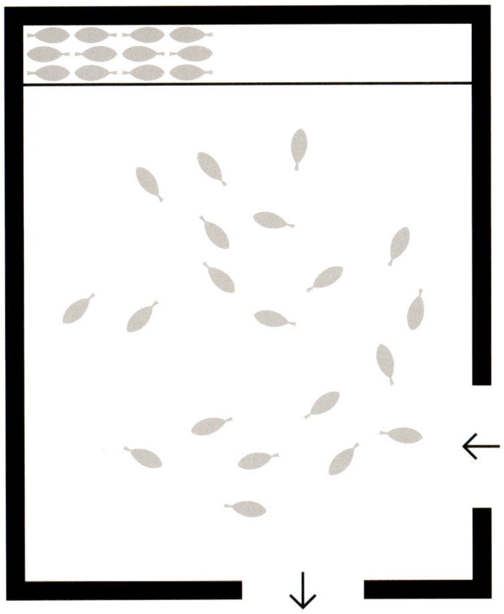

Durch die Verbindung von Wissenschaft, Technologie und Kunst wird diese Vision lebendig. FLOCK OF nutzt eine präzise Choreografie aus Physik, Mechanik und digitaler Steuerung, um ein immersives Erlebnis zu schaffen. Jeder mit Helium gefüllte Ballon ist mit einer speziellen Steuerplatine ausgestattet, die seine Position im Raum erfasst und seine Bewegungen koordiniert – ein harmonisches Zusammenspiel von Algorithmen und ästhetischer Dynamik.

Am Ende bleibt eine Erfahrung, die sich der klaren Einordnung entzieht. FLOCK OF lädt dazu ein, sich in dieser multisensorischen Welt zu verlieren und die Grenze zwischen Wirklichkeit und Imagination neu zu denken.

AN INTERPLAY OF ART, TECHNOLOGY AND SCIENCE DESIGNED TO MAKE THE INTERRELATION OF THE WORLD VISIBLE.

The result of all of this is an experience that is difficult to categorise. FLOCK OF invites visitors to lose themselves in this multisensory world and to rethink the boundaries between reality and the imagination.

PUBLIC

THE 1000 HANDS PROJECT – KINETIC WALL

SOLIDSENSE GMBH, STUTTGART

Location
Deutsches Museum Nürnberg – Das Zukunftsmuseum, Nuremberg

Client
Deutsches Museum Nürnberg – Das Zukunftsmuseum, Nuremberg

Month / Year
August 2024 (Launch)

Duration
Permanent

Dramaturgy / Artists / Show acts
PLAN VALLEY GmbH, Stuttgart

Direction / Coordination / Architecture / Design / Construction
SOLIDSENSE GmbH, Stuttgart

Photos
Milo Wiersdorff, Stuttgart

EINE KINETIC WALL VERBINDET TECHNOLOGISCHE INNOVATION MIT KÜNSTLERI-SCHER FREIHEIT.

Das Foyer des Deutschen Museums Nürnberg sollte eine innovative Bespielung erhalten. Mit SOLIDSENSE entstand die Idee einer Kinetic Wall. Statt einer klassischen Monitorinstallation sollte ein lebendiges, kinetisches Kunstwerk entstehen, das die Verbindung von physischer und digitaler Welt erlebbar macht. Als digitale Leinwand sollte sie zugleich wechselnde künstlerische Bespielungen ermöglichen.

Die Kinetic Wall wurde als sich stetig veränderndes Kunstwerk konzipiert, das in verschiedenen Inszenierungen immer neue visuelle Erlebnisse schafft. Die Erstbespielung durch das Künstlerkollektiv PlanValley nahm das Prinzip des Simulationsspiels „Game of Life" auf und inszenierte eine fortlaufende, dynamische Entwicklung aus Licht, Bewegung und Interaktion. Zur Winterzeit verwandelte sich die Wand in ein poetisches Schneetreiben.

The aim of the project was to realise an innovative animation of the foyer of the Deutsches Museum Nürnberg (German Museum Nuremberg), resulting in the idea of a kinetic wall in collaboration with SOLIDSENSE. Instead of a conventional monitor installation, it was intended to be a vibrant, kinetic work of art that made it possible to experience the combination of the physical and digital world. The digital screen was also designed to enable alternating artistic animations.

The kinetic wall was conceived as a constantly changing work of art, continuously providing new visual experiences through a variety of scenarios. The first animation by the art collective PlanValley incorporated the principle of the simulation game "Game of Life" and presented a continuous, dynamic evolution of light, movement and interaction. During the winter, the wall transformed into the poetic drifting of snow.

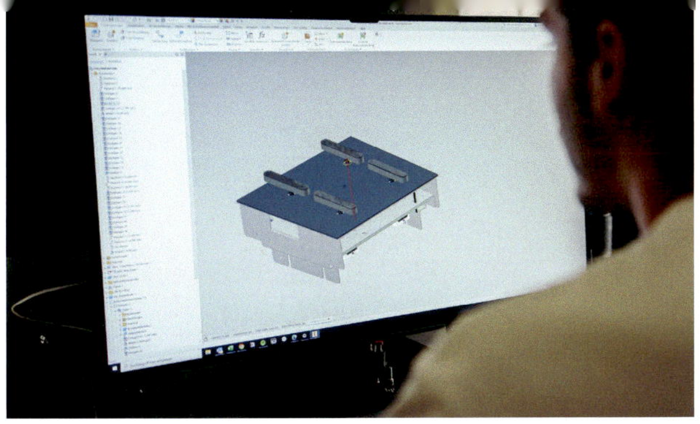

Die Installation besteht aus 196 individuell steuerbaren, rotierenden Zeigern mit je sieben videofähigen LEDs auf einer 2 mal 2 Meter großen schwarzen Grundfläche. Präzise Mechanik, ausgefeilte Elektronik und eine maßgeschneiderte Software ermöglichen einen fließenden Wechsel der visuellen Darstellungen und eine einzigartige Kombination aus physischer Bewegung und digitaler Steuerung. Die Ansteuerung erfolgt über das ArtNet-Protokoll, sodass Digitalkünstler:innen weltweit Inhalte live auf die Wand übertragen können. Ein Digital Twin erlaubt eine ortsunabhängige Voransicht und Programmierung der Bespielung. Durch den modularen Aufbau lassen sich defekte Elemente nahezu werkzeuglos austauschen, wodurch die langfristige Funktionalität gesichert ist.

Die hybride Nutzung der Kinetic Wall ermöglicht ein globales Kunstnetzwerk und schafft neue Formen der Kollaboration – auch KI-generierte Inhalte und Sensorik ließen sich integrieren. Sie steht somit für eine neue Dimension digital-kinetischer Kunst und verbindet technologische Innovation mit künstlerischer Freiheit.

The installation consists of 196 individually controllable, rotating hands, each with seven video-compatible LEDs, on a two-by-two-metre black surface. Precise mechanics, sophisticated electronics and customised software enable the smooth alternation of the visual presentations and a unique combination of physical movement and digital control through the ArtNet protocol, so that digital artists worldwide can transmit live content to the wall. A digital twin allows the animation to be previewed and programmed from any location. Due to the modular structure, faulty elements can be replaced almost without any tools, ensuring long-term functionality.

A KINETIC WALL COMBINES TECHNOLOGICAL INNOVATION AND ARTISTIC FREEDOM.

The hybrid use of the kinetic wall enables a global art network and fosters new forms of collaboration. It is also possible to integrate AI-generated content and sensors. It therefore represents a new dimension of digital-kinetic art and brings together technological innovation and artistic freedom.

PUBLIC

EX·LIBRIS

STUDIOPRODUKTION EVENT MEDIA HDM, STUTTGART

Location
Hochschule der Medien, Stuttgart

Client
Hochschule der Medien, Stuttgart

Month / Year
July 2024

Duration
6 days

Awards
Bronze (Space – Exhibition) at CommAward Talents 2024

Dramaturgy
M. Anselem; M. Löffler; P. Heinrich; I. Kaub

Direction / Coordination
S. Hanna; A. Dreshaj; T. Matula

Architecture / Design
P. Heinrich; M. Löffler; M. Anselem; B. Ziegler; I. Kaub; J. Schmid; J. Müller; L. Krauß

Graphics
T. Matula; S. Hoffmann; M. Anselem

Lighting
S. Hanna; A. Hertling; J. Müller

Media / Films
M. Kampa

Music
T. von Collani; Z. Müller; L. Krauß

Decoration
B. Ziegler; E. Hund; E. Dana; F. Mylius; I. Kaub; J. Müller; L. Krauß; M. Anselem; M. Ehrler; M. Löffler; P. Heinrich; S. Hoffmann

Construction
S. Hanna; A. Dreshaj; T. Matula; B. Ziegler; E. Hund; E. Dana; F. Mylius; I. Kaub; J. Schmid; J. Müller; L. Krauß; M. Anselem; M. Ehrler; M. Löffler; P. Heinrich; S. Hoffmann

Others
T. Matula, A. Hertling, J. Schmid (Media technology) / Programming)

Photos
HdM, Studioproduktion Event Media, Stuttgart

AN INTERACTIVE EXPERIENCE COMBINES FAIRY TALES WITH ESCAPE ROOM SCENARIOS AND DESIGN THAT MAKES A STATEMENT.

Die Natur ist magisch – doch sie ist bedroht. Dieses zentrale Motiv stand hinter dem immersiven Erlebnis „Magischer Wald", das von Studierenden der Hochschule der Medien (HdM) entwickelt wurde. Inspiriert von Märchen und Escape-Room-Mechaniken, verband das Projekt Gestaltung mit einer Botschaft: Der Mensch selbst gefährdet seinen Lebensraum – nur durch aktives Handeln kann das Gleichgewicht gewahrt werden.

Die Reise begann in einer antiken Bibliothek. Lebendige Bücher und sprechende Gemälde erzählten die Geschichte der Figur Billy, die aus ihrem Buch fiel und im magischen Wald für Chaos sorgte. Doch Billys Streiche waren mehr als nur verspielte Einfälle – sie symbolisierten den menschlichen Einfluss auf die Umwelt. Nun lag es an den Besucher:innen, den Wald zu retten und seine Magie zu bewahren ...

Nature is magical – but it is under threat. This was the key motif behind the immersive experience entitled "Magical Forest", which was developed by students at the Media University (HdM). The project was inspired by fairy tales and escape room mechanics, combining design with a message: Humanity itself is endangering its habitat – this can only be compensated through active intervention.

EIN INTERAKTIVES ERLEBNIS VERBINDET MÄRCHEN MIT ESCAPE ROOM UND GESTALTUNG MIT BOTSCHAFT.

The journey started in an ancient library. Living books and talking paintings told the story of the character Billy, who fell out of a book and caused chaos in the magical forest. However, Billy's antics were more than just playful ideas – they symbolised human influence on the environment. It was now up to the visitors to save the forest and preserve its magic ...

After being led into the library, the participants stepped into the fairytale forest – a world of luminous mushrooms, moving flowers and interactive trees. Four tasks had to be mastered. These included lifting a stone out of a well by pulling hoists simultaneously and putting the magic mushrooms in the right frequency using touch. Real books, moving images and the light and sound design generated a setting that brought together technology and storytelling. It consisted of interactive mechanical elements, combined with digital interfaces with the help of hidden sensors, LED walls, fragrance dispensers and specially developed mechanics realised through 3D printing.

Combining the leisurely narrative style of a fairy tale with the contemporary dynamics of an escape room presented a particular challenge. It was about creating a balance between intuitive usability, self-explanatory interactions and a system that was capable of maintaining tension as well as immersion.

Nach der Einführung in der Bibliothek betraten die Teilnehmer:innen den Märchenwald – eine Welt aus leuchtenden Pilzen, beweglichen Blumen und interaktiven Bäumen. Vier Aufgaben mussten bewältigt werden. Mal galt es, einen Stein aus einem Brunnen zu heben, indem Seilzüge simultan betätigt wurden; mal mussten die magischen Pilze mit Berührungen in die richtige Frequenz versetzt werden. Echte Bücher, bewegte Bilder und das Licht-und-Sound-Design erzeugten ein Setting, das Technologie und Storytelling verband. Es bestand aus interaktiven mechanischen Elementen, kombiniert mit digitalen Schnittstellen mit versteckten Sensoren, LED-Wänden, Duftdispensern und eigens entwickelten Mechaniken, die durch 3D-Druck realisiert wurden.

Eine besondere Herausforderung war es, die gemächliche Erzählweise eines Märchens mit der zeitlichen Dynamik eines Escape Rooms zu vereinen. Hier galt es, ein Gleichgewicht zu schaffen zwischen intuitiver Bedienbarkeit, selbst erklärenden Interaktionen und einem System, das in der Lage war, sowohl Spannung als auch Immersion zu bewahren.

AFD-VERBOT

PUBLIC

ADENAUER SRP+ – COMMAND POST OF CIVIL SOCIETY

ZENTRUM FÜR POLITISCHE SCHÖNHEIT, BERLIN

Location
Roadshow throughout Germany

Client
Civil society (Over 10,000 investors)

Month / Year
January 2025 (Launch)

Duration
Ongoing – at least until AfD prohibition

Awards
Winner of 5 general inspections

Dramaturgy / Direction / Coordination / Architecture / Design / Graphics / Lighting / Media / Films / Technology
Zentrum für Politische Schönheit, Berlin

Photos
Zentrum für Politische Schönheit, Berlin

EINE MOBILE BÜHNE, AUSSTELLUNG UND LAUTSTARKE BARRIKADE GEGEN RECHTS-EXTREMISMUS.

Since January 2025, an exceptional vehicle has been a talking point: an extensively converted prisoner transporter, the "Adenauer SRP+". What is behind it is an artistic-political project by the artist collective "Zentrum für Politische Schönheit" (ZPS, Political Beauty). The aim: to draw attention with over 2400 pieces of evidence for the anti-constitutional stance of AfD and through effective technology to the "overwhelming burden of proof" and bring about a prohibition of AfD.

Seit Januar 2025 macht ein außergewöhnliches Fahrzeug von sich reden: ein aufwendig umgebauter Gefangenentransporter, der „Adenauer SRP+". Dahinter verbirgt sich ein künstlerisch-politisches Projekt des Künstlerkollektivs „Zentrum für Politische Schönheit" (ZPS). Das Ziel: Mit über 2.400 Beweisen für die Verfassungsfeindlichkeit der AfD und effektvoller Technik auf die „erdrückende Beweislast" lautstark aufmerksam machen und ein Verbot der AfD erwirken.

A MOBILE STAGE, EXHIBITION AND A LOUD PROTEST AGAINST RIGHT-WING EXTREMISM.

Der Adenauer SRP+ ist für das ZPS weit mehr als ein Transportmittel. Er ist Bühne, Ausstellung, Barrikade – und dient ganz unterschiedlichen Zwecken: Erstens als Bühne und Unterstützung des zivilen Protests, zweitens als mobiles TV- und Streamingstudio und drittens als Tool, um Veranstaltungen der Rechtsextremen zu stören. Mal fungiert der Adenauer als mobile Protestbühne oder empfängt Politker:innen, mal unterbricht er Veranstaltungen der AfD mit Faktenprojektionen, mal streamt er live in soziale Netzwerke. Was bleibt, sind Bilder: von Begegnungen, Debatten, Widerstand. Und eine Botschaft, die in den Köpfen bleibt und von sämtlichen Leitmedien aufgegriffen wurde.

For ZPS, the Adenauer SRP+ is far more than a means of transport. It is a stage, exhibition, protest – and serves a wide range of purposes: firstly, as a stage and to support the civil protest, secondly as a mobile TV and streaming studio, and thirdly as a tool to disrupt extreme right events. Sometimes the Adenauer acts as a mobile protest stage or it receives politicians, sometimes it disrupts AfD events with fact projections, sometimes it streams live on social networks. What remains are images: of encounters, debates, resistance. And a message that remains imprinted on the mind and has been taken up by leading media.

The Adenauer SRP+, originally planned as a temporary project until the federal election, soon became a symbol of active and determined resistance against right-wing extremism. In view of the still increasing popularity of AfD, it will now be transferred permanently to "regular duty". This has been made possible by over 10,000 people who supported the project through crowdfunding – and can continue to do so on www.der-adenauer.de.

Ursprünglich als temporäres Projekt bis zur Bundestagswahl geplant, wurde der Adenauer SRP+ in kürzester Zeit zu einem Symbol für aktiven und entschlossenen Widerstand gegen Rechtsextremismus. Angesichts der weiterhin wachsenden Popularität der AfD wird er nun dauerhaft in den „Regeldienst" übergehen. Möglich gemacht haben das über 10.000 Menschen, die das Projekt per Crowdfunding unterstützt haben – und auch weiterhin auf www.der-adenauer.de unterstützen können.

Die Route des Fahrzeugs bestimmt die Community. Vorschläge für Einsätze werden bei „Adenauer Reisen" gesammelt und darauf basierend angefahren – immer dort, wo die Demokratie gerade besonders unter Druck steht. Nicht immer ohne Widerstand: In den ersten Monaten kam es wiederholt zu Auseinandersetzungen mit der Polizei, die den SRP+ beschlagnahmte, kontrollierte und zeitweise auch stilllegte.

Trotzdem bleibt der Wagen auf der Straße. Mit über 15 Polizeikontrollen und fünf technischen Vollabnahmen in kürzester Zeit spricht das ZPS vom „meistgeprüften Fahrzeug Deutschlands" und einer „systematischen Verhinderung von Protest und massiven Eingriffen in die Kunstfreiheit durch die Polizei Berlin". „Die Polizei Berlin wollte Dinge finden, die nicht zulässig sind", so Arne Heyen vom ZPS. „Aber es kam immer zum gleichen Ergebnis: Alles in bester Ordnung."

The vehicle's route is determined by the community. Suggestions for use are gathered by "Adenauer Reisen" ('Adenauer Travels') and are followed on that basis – always where democracy is under particular pressure. Not always without resistance: During the first months there were repeated conflicts with the police, who seized the SRP+, controlled it and sometimes even put it out of action.

Despite this, the vehicle remains on the road. With over 15 police controls and five full technical MOTs within a short space of time, ZPS speaks of the "most tested vehicle in Germany" and a "systematic obstruction of protest and massive interventions into artistic freedom by the Berlin police". "The Berlin police wanted to find things that are prohibited," according to Arne Heyen from ZPS. "But it always led to the same finding: Everything is in order."

Jede Zielgruppe hat unterschiedliche Bedürfnisse und Erwartungen. Dementsprechend sind Eventkonzepte im Idealfall nicht nur auf den Absender, sondern vor allem auf die Empfänger zugeschnitten.

CONSUMERS: VERBRAUCHER ODER KONSUMENTEN, DIE EINE ODER MEHRERE WAREN ODER DIENSTLEISTUNGEN ZUR EIGENEN (PRIVATEN) BEDÜRFNISBEFRIEDIGUNG KÄUFLICH ERWERBEN WOLLEN ODER VIELMEHR SOLLEN. DABEI HANDELT ES SICH MEIST UM NOCH UNBEKANNTE, ABER SCHON INTERESSIERTE PERSONEN, DIE ZU LANGJÄHRIGEN, TREUEN KUNDEN WERDEN KÖNNTEN UND DAMIT DER ABSATZFÖRDERUNG VON UNTERNEHMEN DIENEN.

CONSUMERS

Each target group has different requirements and expectations. Event concepts are therefore ideally not only geared towards the addressor, but especially towards the recipients.

CONSUMERS: CONSUMERS OR USERS ARE THOSE WHO WANT TO OR SHOULD PURCHASE ONE OR SEVERAL PRODUCTS OR SERVICES TO SATISFY THEIR OWN (PRIVATE) REQUIREMENTS. THEY ARE MOSTLY STILL UNKNOWN, BUT ALREADY INTERESTED PERSONS WHO COULD BECOME LONG-STANDING, LOYAL CUSTOMERS AND THEREFORE BENEFIT THE SALES PROMOTION OF THE COMPANY.

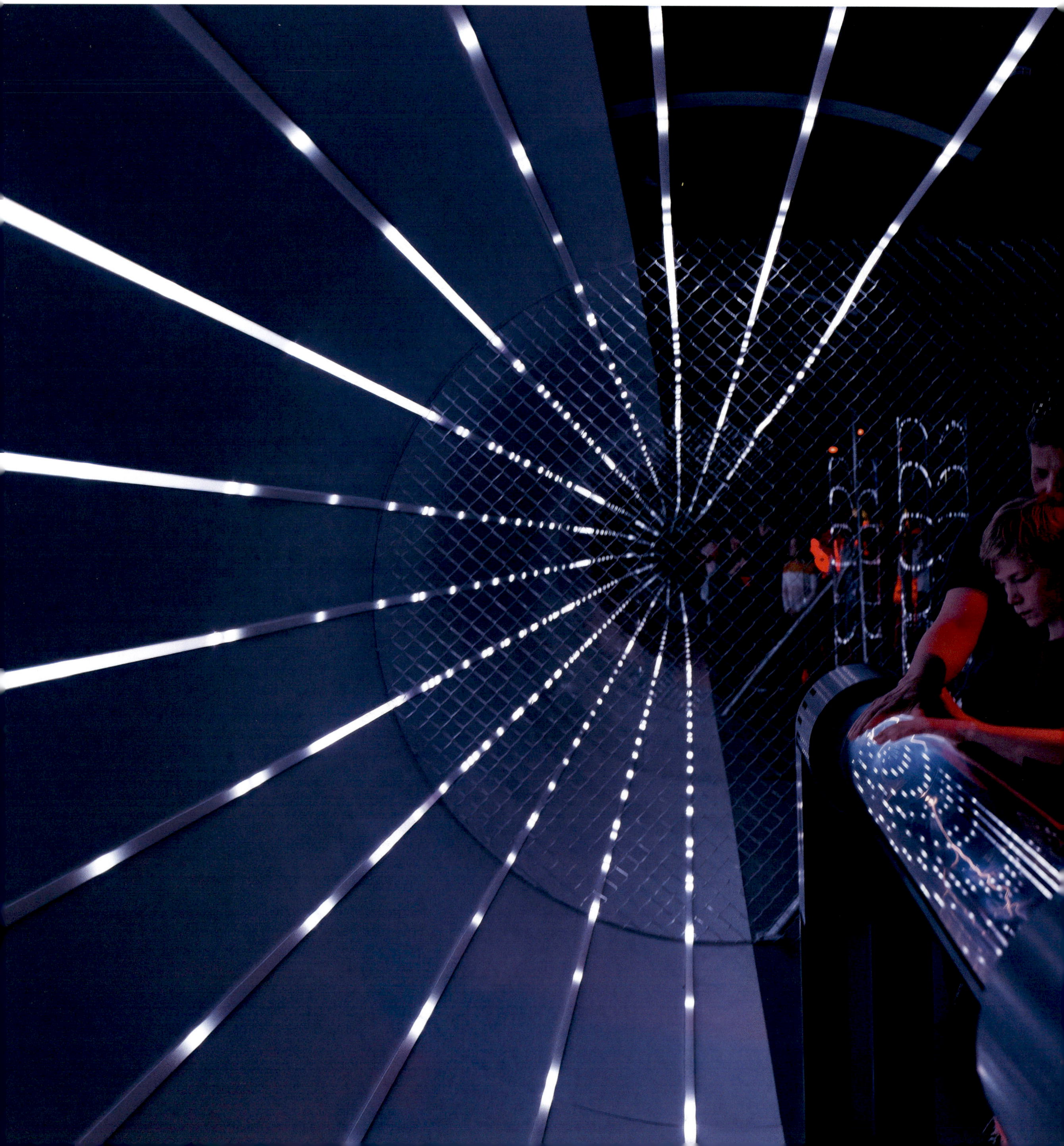

SCIENCE AND EXPERIENCE CENTER – PRIMEO ENERGIE KOSMOS

BELLPRAT PARTNER AG, ZURICH

Location
Science and Experience Center – Primeo Energie Kosmos, Münchenstein

Client
Primeo Energie AG, Münchenstein

Month / Year
January 2023 (Opening)

Duration
Permanent

Awards
Red Dot Award 2023 (Exhibition Design), Gold (Excellence in Brand Strategy and Creation – Brand Communication – User Experience) at German Brand Award 2023; Silver (Space – Exhibition) at CommAwards 2024

Dramaturgy / Direction / Coordination / Architecture / Design / Graphics
Bellprat Partner AG, Zurich

Lighting
atelierstromberg, Cologne

Media / Films / Music
visualsscience.net, Winterthur

Construction
kpm3 AG, Diessenhofen

Others
tebeau – Schniz Scheufler Medieningenieure PartG, Stuttgart (Media planning); auviso AG, Emmenbrücke-Luzern (Lighting and Media Technology); MKT engineering GmbH & Co. KG, Maisach

Photos
Primeo Energie AG, Münchenstein

EIN SCIENCE CENTER VERBINDET EINE INTERAKTIVE ERLEBNISWELT MIT WISSENSCHAFTLICHER BILDUNG.

Primeo Energie Kosmos is a science and experience centre all about the topics of climate and energy. It was established on the occasion of the 125-year company anniversary of Primeo Energie AG. The aim was to create an interesting extra-mural knowledge and learning venue in accordance with the Swiss Curriculum 21 and to convey natural sciences, technology and sustainability interactively.

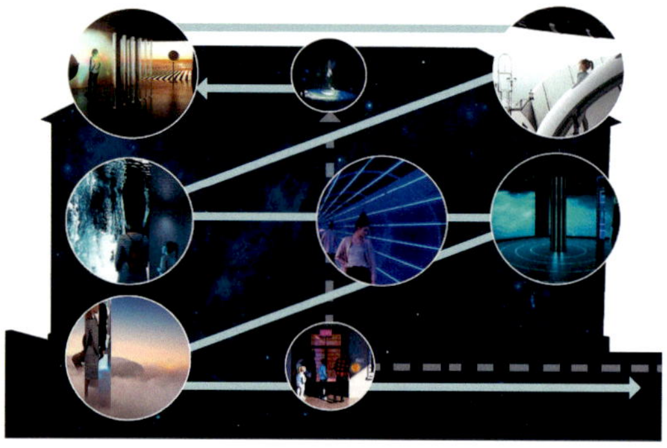

Der Primeo Energie Kosmos ist ein Science- und Erlebniscenter rund um die Themen Klima und Energie. Es enstand anlässlich des 125-jährigen Firmenjubiläums der Primeo Energie AG. Das Ziel war es, einen spannenden Wissens- sowie außerschulischen Lernort gemäß Schweizer Lehrplan 21 zu gestalten. Naturwissenschaften, Technik und Nachhaltigkeit sollten interaktiv vermittelt werden.

Bellprat Partner designed a centre that combines an immersive experience with scientific education. Visitors can experience a variety of important climate and energy phenomena at 17 interactive exhibits. A 45-minute immersive experience show also allows guests to immerse themselves in the fascinating world of energy. On their scheduled and automated circuit, they can feel the power of the sun, climb on a wind turbine, head down into a hydroelectric plant and at the end even walk on clouds.

Bellprat Partner gestaltete ein Zentrum, das ein immersives Erlebnis mit wissenschaftlicher Bildung kombiniert. An 17 interaktiven Exponaten können Besucher:innen verschiedene Phänomene zu wichtigen Klima- und Energiethemen erleben. In einer 45-minütigen immersiven Erlebnisshow tauchen Gäste in die spannende Welt der Energie ein. Auf ihrem getakteten und automatisierten Rundgang spüren sie die Kraft der Sonne, steigen auf ein Windrad, tauchen in ein Wasserkraftwerk hinab und laufen am Ende sogar auf Wolken.

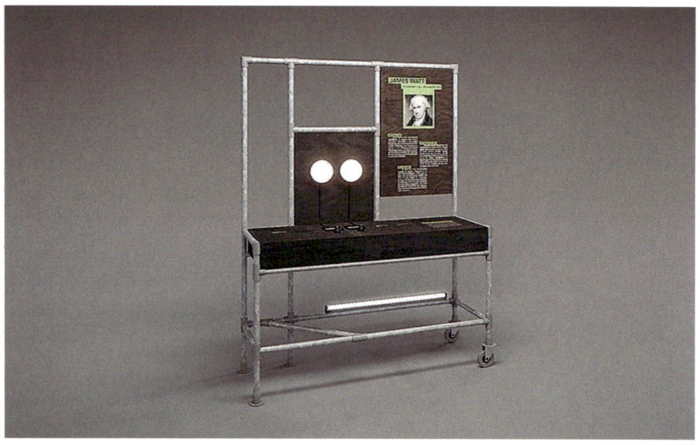

A SCIENCE CENTRE COMBINES AN INTERACTIVE WORLD OF EXPERIENCE WITH SCIENTIFIC EDUCATION.

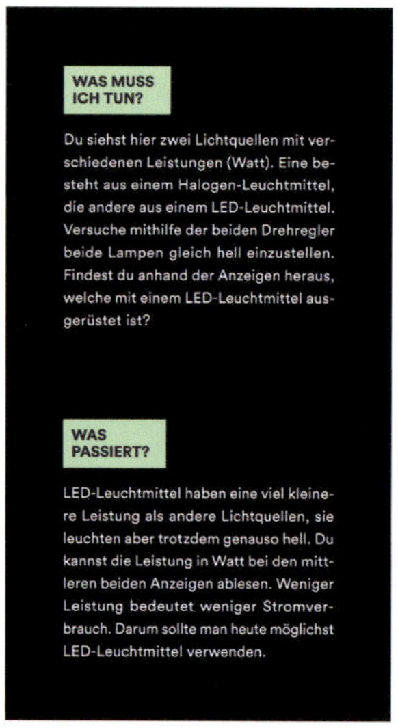

In addition, guided tours, energy shows and didactic workshops, developed in collaboration with Fachhochschule Nordwestschweiz (FHNW – University of Applied Sciences and Arts Northwestern Switzerland) provide more in-depth insights into complex contexts. The contemporary concept is designed to spark interest in STEM subjects in particular among secondary school pupils.

Ergänzend dazu bieten Führungen, Energieshows und didaktische Workshops, entwickelt in Zusammenarbeit mit der Fachhochschule Nordwestschweiz (FHNW), vertiefende Einblicke in komplexe Hintergründe. Mit dem zeitgemäßen Konzept sollen insbesondere Schülerinnen und Schüler der Sekundarstufe für MINT-Fächer begeistert werden.

Das ehemalige Elektrizitätsmuseum (W8) wurde umfassend saniert und beherbergt nun das immersive Erlebniscenter. Ergänzt wird es durch einen architektonisch wegweisenden Neubau (W6), der Raum für das Science Center und die Workshopbereiche schafft. Der Bau orientiert sich am Prinzip der Kreislaufwirtschaft: Die verwendeten Materialien sind größtenteils recycelt, wiederverwendet oder aus nachwachsenden Rohstoffen gefertigt. Ein praktisches Beispiel dafür, was unter dem Stichwort Kreislaufwirtschaft beim Bauen möglich ist.

The former Electricity Museum (W8) was comprehensively renovated and now houses the immersive experience centre. An architecturally pioneering new building (W6) has been added, providing space for the Science Center and the workshop areas. The building is orientated towards the principle of a circular economy: The majority of the materials used are recycled, reused or made of renewable raw materials. It is a practical example of what is possible in construction under the motto of circular economy.

RED BULL'S MR GAME – ARENA DEFENDER

BRIGHT! GMBH, MAINTAL

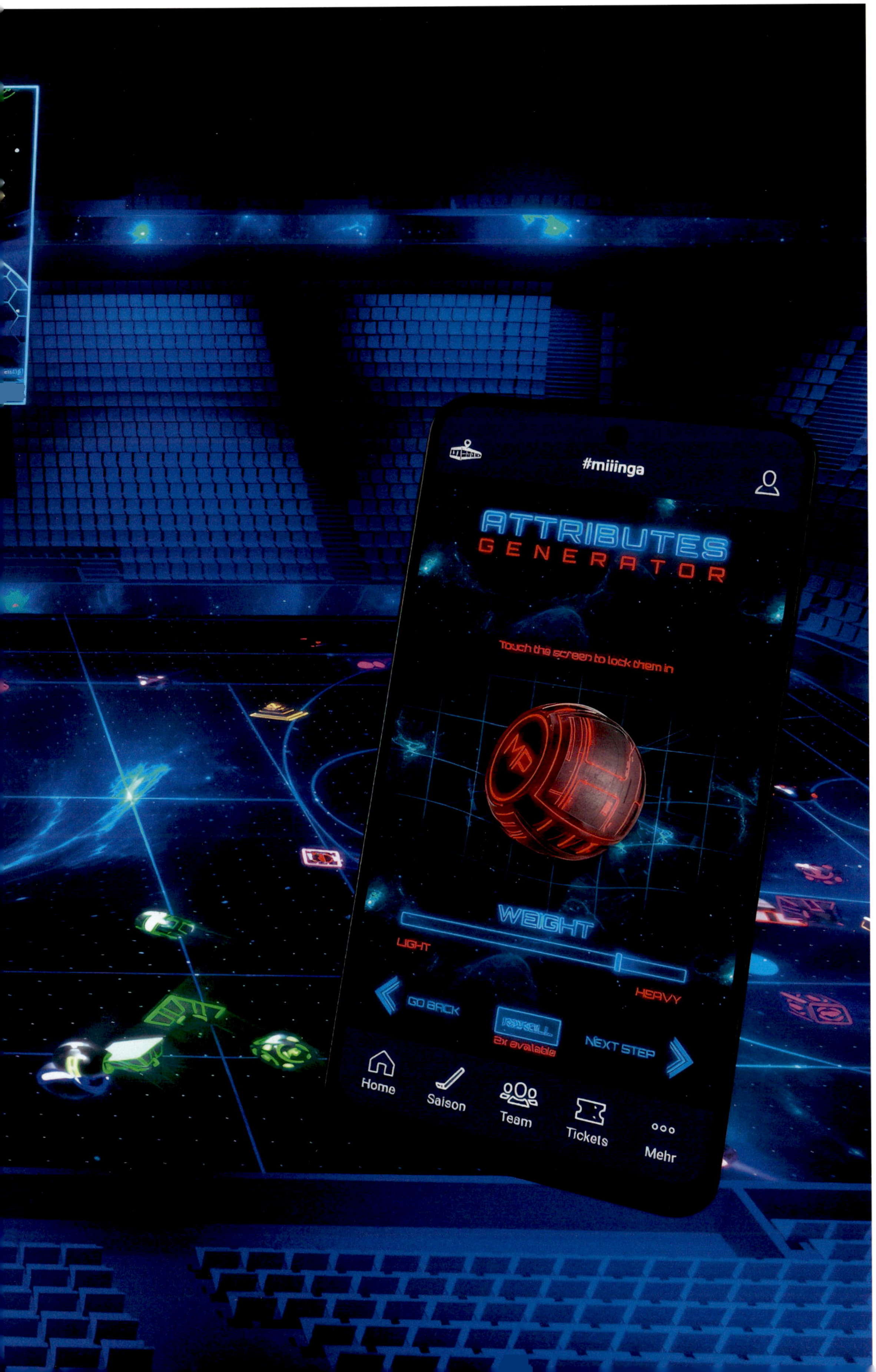

Location
SAP Garden, Munich

Client
EHC Red Bull München, Munich

Month / Year
October 2024 (Launch)

Duration
Permanent

Direction / Coordination
bright! GmbH Michael Giegerich, Maintal

Architecture / Design
bright! GmbH Leon Herche / Thomas Flechel / Vincent Struck, Maintal

Graphics
bright! GmbH Moritz Plath / Fabian Bertoldo, Maintal

Photos
Red Bull München / City-Press, Munich; bright! GmbH, Maintal

Wie erreicht man Tausende Sportfans mit einem packenden, interaktiven Stadionevent? Mit dieser Fragestellung als Ziel entwickelte bright! für Red Bull und das SAP Garden ein interaktives Mixed-Reality-Game: Arena Defender. Ein Spielerlebnis, bei dem aus Zuschauer:innen aktive Mitspieler:innen werden.

EIN DYNAMISCHES MIXED-REALITY-ERLEBNIS MACHT AUS STADION-GÄSTEN AKTIVE MITSPIELER:INNEN.

How can one reach thousands of sports fans with a gripping interactive stadium event? With this question in mind, bright! developed the interactive mixed reality game Arena Defender for Red Bull and the SAP Garden, a game experience in which spectators become active players.

Participants can create their own objects via the Red Bull app and "throw" them into the game, while the players on the ice, wearing mixed reality headsets, try to fend off these objects with virtual shields. The experience is enhanced by means of dynamic gaming elements such as movable portals, laser obstacles and a pachinko mechanism on the LED cube. Objects that fall successfully through the pachinko board and hit a target earn fans loyalty points and the chance to win attractive prizes. The players can follow their objects, are actively incorporated into the process and are therefore emotionally involved with the game.

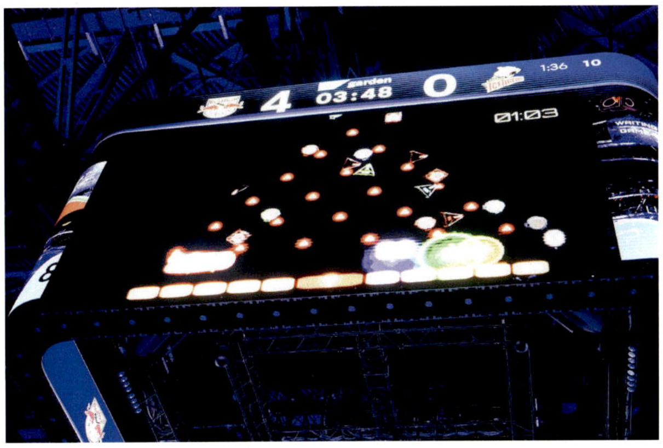

Über die Red Bull App können Teilnehmende eigene Objekte gestalten und ins Spiel „werfen", während die Spieler:innen auf dem Eis mit Mixed-Reality-Headsets versuchen, diese Objekte mit virtuellen Schilden abzuwehren. Das Erlebnis wird durch dynamische Spielelemente wie bewegliche Portale, Laser-Hindernisse und einen Pachinko-Mechanismus auf dem LED-Cube bereichert. Erfolgreich durch das Pachinko-Brett fallende Objekte, die ein Ziel treffen, bringen den Fans Loyalty Points und die Chance auf attraktive Preise. Die Player können ihre Objekte verfolgen, sind aktiv in den Ablauf eingebunden und erleben so eine emotionale Verbindung zum Spiel.

Das Konzept kombiniert Mixed Reality, Echtzeitprojektionen auf dem Eis und eine nahtlose digitale App-Integration. Für die Umsetzung wurden neueste Technologien wie Meta-Quest-3-Headsets, Echtzeit-Simulationen mit Unreal Engine und ein cloudbasiertes Backend über Amazon AWS eingesetzt. Diese technische Verschmelzung ermöglicht es, Tausende parallele Interaktionen zwischen den Fans und den Spieler:innen auf dem Eis zu verarbeiten. Durch die Integration in die Red Bull App und die Verknüpfung mit den Loyalty Points bleiben die Gamer:innen auch nach dem Event mit der Marke verbunden. Ein herausforderndes Projekt, das ein nahtloses Erlebnis schaffen, für ein breites Publikum verständlich, intuitiv und zugleich technologisch präzise und mitreißend sein soll.

STADIUM GUESTS BECOME ACTIVE PLAYERS IN A DYNAMIC MIXED REALITY EXPERIENCE.

The concept combines mixed reality, real-time projections on the ice and a seamless digital app integration. The latest technologies such as Meta-Quest-3 headsets, real-time simulations with Unreal Engine and a cloud-based backend through Amazon AWS were used for the realisation. This blend of technologies made it possible to process thousands of parallel interactions between the fans and the players on the ice. The players remain involved with the brand even after the event through the integration into the Red Bull app and the gathering of loyalty points. It is a challenging project that is intended to create a seamless experience and to be understandable, intuitive and at the same time technologically precise and captivating for a wide public.

SAMSUNG
SmartThings
Smarter leben
mit SmartThings
Erkunde empfohlene SmartThings Erlebnisse
basierend auf deinem Lebensstil und deinen Vorlieben.
smartthings-roadshow.com
SmartThings
Sei smart,
dreh am Rad!
Baue ein nachhaltiges Zuhause mit
SmartThings Energy Partnern
SMA

LYX FESTIVAL

EREIGNISHAUS LIVE-MARKETING, GENOKOM WERBEAGENTUR GMBH, COLOGNE

Location
Koelncongress GmbH, Cologne

Client
Bastei Lübbe AG, Cologne

Month / Year
August 2024

Duration
3 days

Dramaturgy / Direction / Coordination
Bastei Lübbe AG, Cologne; ereignishaus Agentur für Live-Marketing, Cologne

Architecture / Design / Graphics
ereignishaus Agentur für Live-Marketing, Cologne

Graphics
Bastei Lübbe AG, Cologne

Lighting
müllermusic Veranstaltungstechnik GmbH & Co. KG (Lighting & Technology)

Films
TRUE GmbH, Meerbusch

Music
DJ Polly

Artists / Show acts
Around 30 LYX book authors and audio book speakers

Decoration
Ele Anschütz Bühne und Dekoration UG, Cologne (Ground floor stage & decoration); J&B Messe-Design GmbH, Mechernich-Kommern

Catering
Koelncongress Gastronomie GmbH, Cologne

Photos
Juliane Herrmann – Photographie, Cologne

Im Sommer 2024 wurde New-Adult-Literatur, die Bastei Lübbe mit der Marke LYX bedient, mit einem eigenen Festival gefeiert. Vom 2. bis 4. August fand in Köln-Gürzenich das erste LYX-Festival statt. Mehr als 4.000 Besucher:innen nutzten die Gelegenheit, Autor:innen, Hörbuchsprecher:innen und andere Literaturbegeisterte zu treffen. Die Eventplanung und Umsetzung – von der Architektur bis zur Technik – lag in den Händen von ereignishaus.

Das Festival setzte auf Austausch und Interaktion. Lesungen, Talks, Signierstunden und Workshops boten vielseitige Einblicke in das Genre. Eine Chill-out-Area mit Kopfhörer-Lesungen ergänzte das Programm um ruhigere Momente. Am Samstagabend fand die LYX-Party statt, die als geschützter Raum für Begegnungen und Gespräche diente.

A FESTIVAL FOR NEW ADULT LITERATURE – WITH READINGS, TALKS AND EXPERIENCES.

New adult literature, which Bastei Lübbe serves with the trademark LYX, was celebrated with a special festival in summer 2024. The first LYX festival was held from 2 to 4 August in Cologne-Gürzenich. More than 4000 visitors took the opportunity to meet authors, audio book speakers and other literature enthusiasts. The event planning and realisation – from the architecture to the technology – was placed in the capable hands of ereignishaus.

EIN FESTIVAL FÜR NEW-ADULT-LITERATUR – MIT LESUNGEN, AUSTAUSCH UND ERLEBNISSEN.

Die Gestaltung orientierte sich an der LYX-Markenwelt. Zwei detailverliebt gestaltete Themenräume – Icebreaker und Dark Academia – vermittelten atmosphärische Eindrücke aus den Romanwelten. Fotospots, DIY-Areas, eine Talkbühne und dekorative Verkaufsflächen ergänzten das Festival mit abwechslungsreichen Angeboten.

Das Social-Media-Konzept der Veranstaltung lebte vor allem von der Community, die das Festival für Posts, Reels und TikTok-Videos nutzte. Buch-Influencer:innen unterstützen die digitale Dynamik. DIY-Stationen boten kleine Erinnerungsstücke, darunter Armbänder, die den Community-Gedanken stärken sollten.

The festival was all about communication and interaction. Readings, talks, signings and workshops offered a wide array of insights into the genre. The programme was rounded off with quieter moments provided by a chill-out area with readings through headphones. The LYX party took place on the Saturday evening, serving as a place for encounters and conversations.

The design was orientated towards the LYX brand world. Two themed rooms designed with attention to detail – Icebreaker and Dark Academia – conveyed atmospheric impressions of the worlds of the novels. Photo points, DIY areas, a talk podium and decorative sales areas added varied elements to the festival.

The social media concept of the event was driven in particular by the community, which used the festival for posts, reels and TikTok videos. Book influencers supported the digital dynamics, while DIY stations offered little souvenirs, including bracelets, designed to reinforce the community spirit.

kinder
bueno

KINDER BUENO DAYS

RÜCKENWIND MARKENERLEBNIS GMBH, MUNICH

Location
Museumsinsel, Berlin

Client
Ferrero Deutschland GmbH, Frankfurt am Main

Month / Year
August 2024

Duration
3 days

Direction / Coordination / Architecture / Design
RÜCKENWIND MARKENERLEBNIS GmbH, Munich

Graphics / Films
Populär PR GmbH, Munich

Lighting
MDS PAtec Veranstaltungstechnik GmbH, Munich

Photos
Lisa Bach, Berlin

EIN SOMMERLICHES ERLEBNISFORMAT MACHT DAS POSITIVE MARKEN-MINDSET INDIVIDUELL ERLEBBAR.

Im Mittelpunkt des Relaunches von kinder bueno stand die Transformation und Emotionalisierung der Marke. Um das neue „Bueno-Feeling" erfahrbar zu machen und echte „Bueno-Momente" zu schaffen, wurde ein neues Erlebnisformat entwickelt: die „Bueno Days". Ziel war es, die Markenbekanntheit zu steigern, eine tiefere emotionale Bindung zur Marke zu schaffen und insbesondere die Generation Z durch Community-Aktivierung und mediale Verlängerung anzusprechen.

The focal point of the relaunch of kinder bueno was the transformation and emotionalising of the brand. A new experience format called "Bueno Days" was developed in order to provide an experience of the new "bueno feeling" and create true "bueno moments". The aim was to raise awareness of the brand, to forge a deeper emotional connection to the brand and, in particular, to appeal to generation Z through community activation and media reach.

GEMEINSAMER JAHRESAUFTAKT 2025

METZLER VATER, MUNICH

Location
Messe Stuttgart, Paul Horn Halle (Hall 10)

Client
Württembergische Versicherung AG, Kornwestheim

Month / Year
February 2025

Duration
1 day

Dramaturgy / Architecture / Design / Graphics / Decoration / Construction
METZLER VATER, Munich

Direction / Coordination
Kenneth Tschersich, Cologne

Lighting
Neumann&Müller GmbH & Co. KG, Stuttgart

Media / Films
METZLER VATER, Munich; Kniff Projektagentur GbR, Stuttgart

Music
La Diri (Live entertainment); DJane Alegra Cole (DJane)

Artists / Show acts
Steven Gätjen (Moderation); Thilo Schmelzer (Author); Ranga Yogeshwar, Dr. Georg Kofler, Hanno Höhn (Keynote panels)

Catering
Aramark Restaurations GmbH, Stuttgart

Photos
Andreas Martin, Stuttgart

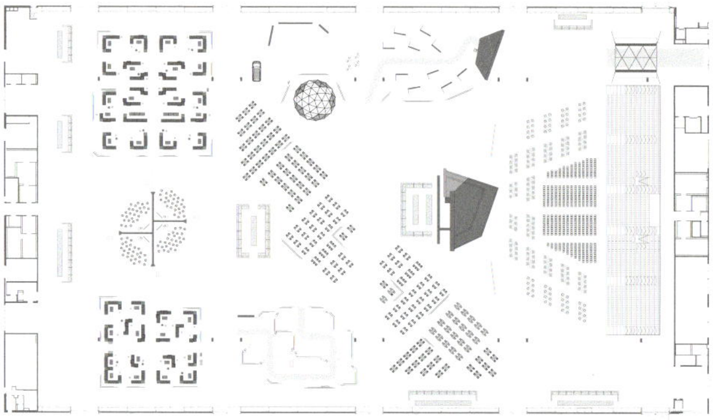

EIN JAHRESAUFTAKT MIT DIVERSEN FORMATEN FÜR WISSENSVERMITTLUNG, INSPIRATION UND AUSTAUSCH.

Der Jahresauftakt 2025 der Württembergischen Versicherung fand am historischen Gründungsort in Stuttgart statt – fast 200 Jahre später. Unter dem Motto „Zukunft gestalten – Transformation als Chance" kamen Kolleg:innen aus ganz Deutschland zusammen, um die inhaltlichen Schwerpunkte und Herausforderungen des Jahres 2025 kennenzulernen und sich motivieren zu lassen. Der Jahresauftakt sollte nicht nur ein motivierter Start in das neue Jahr, sondern auch eine Plattform für Austausch, Wertschätzung, Inspiration und intensive Wissensvermittlung sein.

The Württembergische Versicherung kicked off the year 2025 at its historical foundation site in Stuttgart – almost 200 years on. Under the motto "Shaping the future – transformation as an opportunity", colleagues from all around Germany came together to get to know the key topics and challenges for 2025. It was intended to be not only a motivating start to the new year but also a platform for communication, appreciation, inspiration, and avid knowledge sharing.

KICKING OFF THE YEAR WITH A VARIETY OF FORMATS FOR COMMUNICATION, KNOWLEDGE SHARING AND INSPIRATION.

Das Event von METZLER VATER setzte auf ein interaktives Format, das feste Programmpunkte mit individuell gestaltbaren Elementen kombinierte und den überregionalen Austausch förderte. Die Main Stage bildete den zentralen Anker: Hier fanden die Eröffnung, eine inspirierende Keynote und eine Paneldiskussion statt, die mit einer Abendveranstaltung endete. Ergänzend dazu gab es themenspezifische Bereiche, die vielfältige Erlebnisse boten: einen Dome, Masterclasses zu verschiedenen Themen sowie einen Experience Walk.

Das visuelle Konzept der Veranstaltung wurde durch das Motiv des Markenclaims „Fels in der Brandung" inspiriert. Polygonale Formen in der Gestaltung von Main Stage, Raumtrennern und weiteren Elementen spiegelten dieses Thema wider, während die Lichtstimmung in den Corporate-Farben der Württembergischen Versicherung dramaturgisch auf die jeweiligen Programmpunkte abgestimmt war. Eine durchdachte Planung ermöglichte einen intuitiven Guestflow der rund 2.000 Teilnehmer:innen, sodass alle Gäste die vielfältigen Angebote reibungslos nutzen konnten.

The event by METZLER VATER was based on an interactive format that combined fixed programme elements with some that could be created individually and that encouraged transregional communication. The central anchor was the main stage, where the opening, an inspiring keynote and a panel discussion were held, ending with an evening event. In addition, there were themed areas that offered a variety of experiences: a dome, masterclasses on a range of topics, as well as an Experience Walk.

The visual concept of the event was inspired by the motif of the brand claim "Solid as a rock". Polygonal forms in the design of the main stage, room dividers and other elements reflected this theme, while the lighting atmosphere in the corporate colours of Württembergische Versicherung harmonised dramaturgically with the respective programme items. Well thought out planning enabled an intuitive and smooth guest flow of approximately 2000 participants around the various stations.

Biella

LYRECO UNBOXED – SUSTAINABILITY CONFERENCE AS A DIALOGUE PLATFORM

STANDING OVATION AG, ZURICH

Location
Umwelt Arena Schweiz, Spreitenbach

Client
Lyreco Switzerland AG, Dietikon

Month / Year
January 2024

Duration
1 day

Awards
Gold (Best Corporate Event) at BrandEx 2025; Silver (Best Corporate Event) at Xaver-Award 2024

Dramaturgy / Direction / Coordination / Architecture / Design / Artists / Show acts
standing ovation AG, Zurich

Graphics
Sergeant AG, Zurich

Lighting / Media
smARTec Veranstaltungstechnik AG, Aarau

Decoration / Construction
Brogleworks AG, Spreitenbach

Catering
Dinnercatering GmbH, Zurich

Photos
Inbound Production GmbH, Zurich

EIN OFFENER BRANCHENDIALOG FÜR DIE GEMEINSAME ENTWICKLUNG NACHHALTIGER LÖSUNGEN.

Lyreco, ein Anbieter von Arbeitsplatzprodukten, hat sich zum Ziel gesetzt, seine Nachhaltigkeitsaktivitäten klarer zu positionieren und den Dialog innerhalb der Branche zu stärken. Bestehende Programme und Maßnahmen sollten durch eine partizipative Plattform ergänzt werden, die eine glaubwürdige Auseinandersetzung mit ökologischen und sozialen Herausforderungen ermöglicht. standing ovation entwickelte dafür das Format Lyreco Unboxed – eine Plattform, die Kunden, Produzenten und Experten zusammenbringt, um gemeinsam Lösungen für eine nachhaltigere Zukunft zu entwickeln.

Lyreco, a supplier of workplace products, set itself the aim of positioning its sustainability activities more clearly and of fostering dialogue within the industry. Existing programmes and measures were to be supplemented by a participatory platform that enabled credible solutions to ecological and social challenges to be put forward. The agency standing ovation developed the Lyreco Unboxed format for this purpose – a platform that brings customers, producers and experts together to develop joint solutions in the interests of a more sustainable future.

AN OPEN INDUSTRY DIALOGUE ABOUT THE JOINT DEVELOPMENT OF SUSTAINABLE SOLUTIONS.

YUUKI – AN AI EXPERIENCE

ONTO[STORY] GMBH – OFFICE FOR TRANSFORMATION & STORYTELLING, COLOGNE

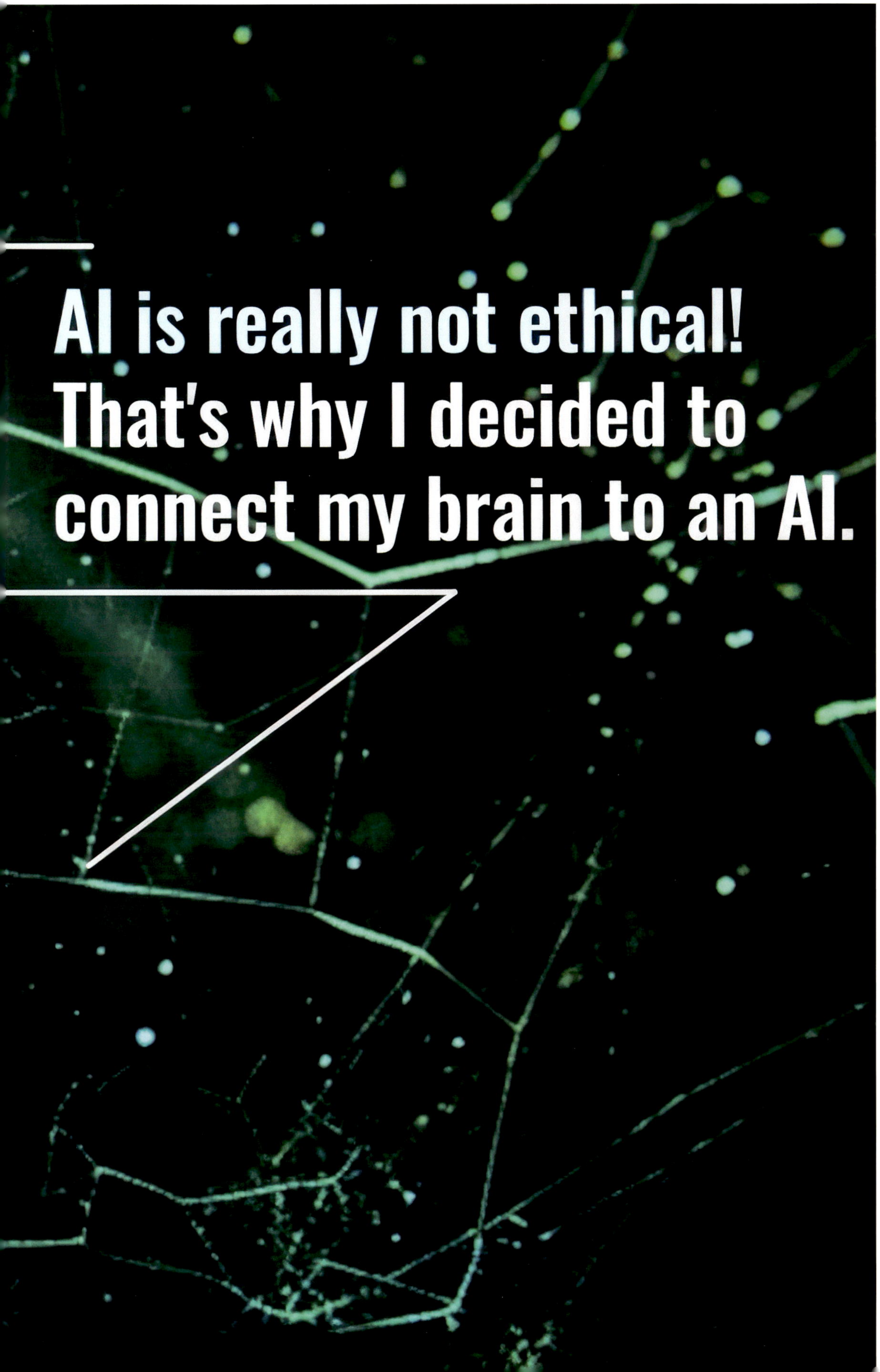

Location
Hotel Berlin, Berlin

Client
Takeda Pharma Vertrieb GmbH & Co. KG, Berlin

Month / Year
April 2024

Duration
2 days

Awards
Gold (Video Storytelling) at Galaxy Awards 2024; Gold (Use of Artificial Intelligence) at Bea World Awards 2024; Gold (Internal Communication) at PR Report Awards 2024; Gold Medal (Events) at Montreux Awards 2025; Silver (Best Creation, Innovation and Discovery) & Bronze (Best Community Engagement) at ICE Awards Europe 2024; Bronze (Best Internal Communications During a Brand Development Project) at Transform Awards Europe 2025

Direction / Coordination
onto[story] Petra Lammers, Cologne

Lighting
Jan-Christoph Hermann, Gründau

Media
BILDQUADRAT GmbH, Dusseldorf

Music
Matt Flores, Dusseldorf

Others
EXCIT3D GmbH, Solingen

Photos
onto[story] GmbH – Office for Transformation & Storytelling, Cologne

EIN AVATAR ALS TESTIMONIAL, TEAMMITGLIED UND INTER-AKTIVES FORMAT FÜR EINE NEUE LERNKULTUR MIT KI.

Künstliche Intelligenz revolutioniert die Arbeitsweise in Unternehmen und ermöglicht eine effizientere Nutzung von Ressourcen. Doch die rasante Entwicklung stellt traditionelle Lernmethoden vor neue Herausforderungen. Statt starrer Schulungsformate braucht es eine Lernkultur, die auf Neugier, Zusammenarbeit und den Austausch individueller Expertise setzt – unabhängig von Hierarchien.

Artificial intelligence is revolutionising the ways companies work and enabling a more efficient use of resources. However, its rapid development is presenting traditional learning methods with new challenges. Instead of rigid training formats, a learning culture is required that is based on curiosity, cooperation and the sharing of individual expertise – independent of hierarchies.

In order to foster this change at Takeda Pharma, onto[story] developed an interactive format that makes it possible to experience the use of AI in everyday working life in a playful manner. The idea was to use AI not only as a topic but also as content and as a method. The centrepiece was the virtual protagonist Yuuki – a digital avatar that acted as a testimonial, storytelling character and expert. She created a collaborative learning environment as a gamified live escape room experience and encouraged the participants to use AI tools. Diversity played a central role in this: the open, interactive approach resulted in a forum for communication and joint discoveries. The aim was to treat AI not only as a topic but also to anchor it as an integral part of the learning process.

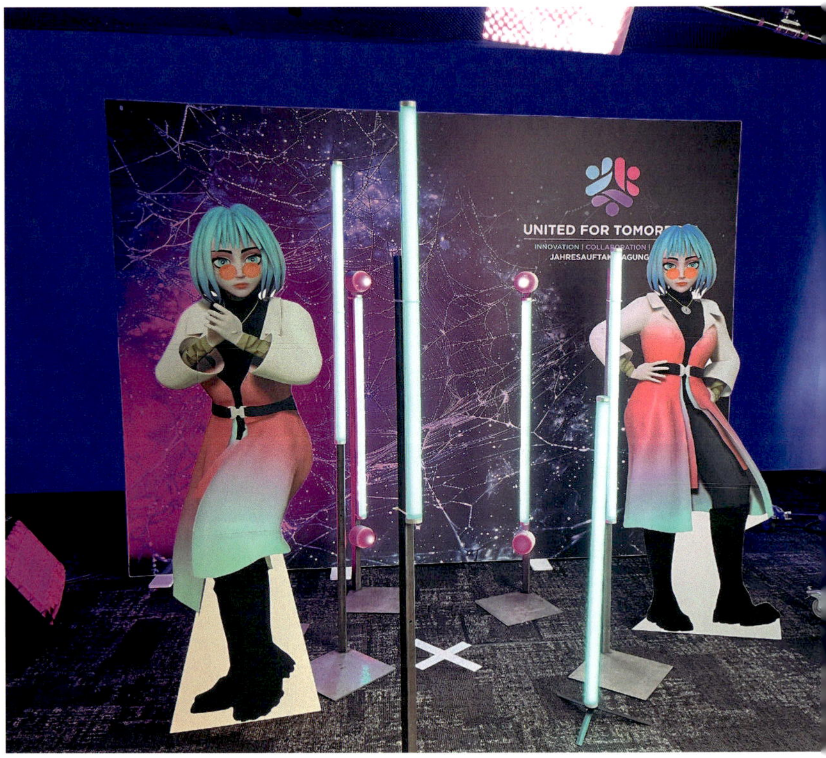

AN AVATAR AS A TESTIMONIAL, TEAM MEMBER AND INTERACTIVE FORMAT FOR A NEW LEARNING CULTURE WITH AI.

Um diese Veränderung bei Takeda Pharma zu fördern, entwickelte onto[story] ein interaktives Format, das den Einsatz von KI im Arbeitsalltag auf spielerische Weise erlebbar macht. Die Idee war, KI nicht nur als Thema, sondern auch als Inhalt und Methode zu nutzen. Herzstück war die virtuelle Protagonistin Yuuki – ein digitaler Avatar, der als Testimonial, Storytelling-Figur und Expertin agierte. In einem gamifizierten Live-Escape-Room-Erlebnis schuf sie eine kollaborative Lernumgebung und motivierte die Teilnehmer:innen, KI-Tools zu nutzen. Diversität spielte dabei eine zentrale Rolle: Durch den offenen, interaktiven Ansatz entstand ein Raum für Austausch und gemeinsames Entdecken. Ziel war es, KI nicht nur als Thema zu behandeln, sondern sie als integralen Bestandteil des Lernprozesses zu verankern.

Yuuki wurde mithilfe einer Motion-Capture-KI-App entwickelt und interagierte sowohl live als auch virtuell mit den Teilnehmenden. Sie hielt eine virtuelle Keynote, moderierte Diskussionen und führte über 400 Mitarbeitende durch ein Szenario, das die Zusammenarbeit und den kreativen Umgang mit KI fördern sollte. Inzwischen ist sie offizielles Teammitglied und treibt die firmeninterne KI-Thematik voran.

Yuukis erster internationaler Auftritt fand im Rahmen einer dreitägigen Schulungssession bei Takeda Schweiz statt. In einem digitalen Event zur Nutzung von KI setzte sie ihren Escape Room erstmals vollständig virtuell um. Eine neue, interaktive Lernerfahrung für über 2.000 Teilnehmende aus Europa, den USA und Kanada.

Yuuki was developed with the help of a motion capture AI app and interacted both live and virtually with the participants. She presented a virtual keynote, moderated discussions and guided over 400 employees through a scenario designed to promote cooperation and the creative handling of AI. She is now an official team member and drives the in-house use of AI forwards.

Yuuki's first international presence was as part of a three-day training session at Takeda Switzerland. She realised her escape room completely virtually for the first time at a digital event about the use of AI. The result was a new, interactive learning experience for over 2000 participants from Europe, the USA and Canada.

PEOPLE.
POWER.
PASSION.

DIGITAL X – INNOVATION, INSPIRATION, IMPACT

VOK DAMS WORLDWIDE, WUPPERTAL

Location
From Rudolfplatz to Mediapark, Cologne

Client
Deutsche Telekom, Bonn

Month / Year
September 2024

Duration
Several days

Overall direction & dramaturgy
VOK DAMS worldwide, Wuppertal

Direction / Artist management
M. Regie GmbH & Co KG, Eschweiler; Papilio Entertainment, Wiesbaden; Eckelmann + Rettig GmbH, Berlin

Architecture / Design
PRODUCTION OFFICE POE GmbH, Berlin; FRAMEWORK GmbH, Cologne (Planning offices)

Media
360Media GmbH, Cologne; Elberfeld Kreation GmbH & Co. KG, Wuppertal; Capture Media GmbH, Dusseldorf

Technology
Neumann&Müller GmbH & Co. KG, Neuhausen a. d. Fildern; kölnton rental GmbH, Cologne; Media Spectrum GmbH & Co. KG, Willich; AVE Audio Visual Equipment GmbH, Bergisch Gladbach; Kuchem Konferenz Technik GmbH & Co. KG, Königswinter

Catering
lemonpie Eventcatering GmbH, Münstereifel; Granny's Gbr, Cologne

Construction
WRCK Raumkonzepte GmbH und Co. KG, Bocholt; KLARTEXT GME GmbH, Willich; Neptunus GmbH, Dusseldorf / atlive eventtechnik GmbH, Hilden (Tents); Nüssli GmbH, Cologne (Stands)

Others
Party Rent Franchise GmbH, Ober-Mörlen (Rental furniture); K16 GmbH, Hamburg (PPT Design); IBIT GmbH, Bonn / Special Security Services Deutschland SSSD GmbH, Bergheim (Security); ADITUS GmbH, Hanover (Ticketing); LiveVoice GmbH, Salzburg (Interpreting technology)

Photos
VOK DAMS worldwide, Wuppertal; Deutsche Telekom, Bonn

DIGITAL-FESTIVAL MIT 50.000 BESUCHERN UND VIELFÄLTIGEN FORMATEN FÜR INFORMATION UND ERLEBNIS.

DIGITAL X is a digitisation initiative and a Deutsche Telekom festival. It has been addressing trends, developments and discussions regarding digital topics since 2018. For the first time in 2024, VOK DAMS as the lead agency took on the realisation, organisation, logistics and participation administration of the whole event under the motto "Ready for Impact".

Die DIGITAL X ist eine Digitalisierungsinitiative und ein Festival der Deutschen Telekom. Seit 2018 beschäftigt sie sich mit Trends, Entwicklungen und Austausch rund um digitale Themen. 2024 übernahm erstmals VOK DAMS als Leadagentur die Umsetzung, Organisation, Logistik und Teilnehmersteuerung der gesamten Veranstaltung unter dem Motto „Ready for Impact".

Auf rund zwei Millionen Quadratmetern präsentierten sich sechs Bühnen, über 250 Speaker:innen, 300 Partnerunternehmen wie Samsung, Microsoft und Cisco sowie zahlreiche Formate für Austausch, Information und Erfahrung – darunter Masterclasses, Ausstellungen und interaktive Erlebnisräume. Im inhaltlichen Mittelpunkt stand die Frage, wie Digitalisierung konkrete Lösungen für Wirtschaft, Politik und Gesellschaft bieten kann.

Six stages, over 250 speakers, 300 partner companies such as Samsung, Microsoft and Cisco, as well as a range of formats for discussions, information and sharing experience – including masterclasses, exhibitions and interactive spaces – were presented across an area spanning around two million square metres. The focal point of the content was the question of how digitisation can offer concrete solutions for economics, politics and society.

A DIGITAL FESTIVAL WITH 50,000 VISITORS AND A WIDE RANGE OF FORMATS FOR INFORMATION AND EXPERIENCES.

Zentrales Element war der DIGITAL X Cube im MediaPark – ein architektonischer Ankerpunkt mit der „Innovation Gallery", die die neuesten digitalen Innovationen, darunter den AR-Laptop mit einem virtuellen 100-Zoll-Bildschirm und das KI-gestützte Testimonial „Judy", präsentierte.

Darüber hinaus konnten Besucher:innen auf digitale Entdeckungstour durch Köln gehen – bei Formaten wie Guided Tours, Drone Soccer, dem ersten Roboter-Mensch-Flashmob und den vielen Brand Houses der Partnerunternehmen.

The DIGITAL X Cube in the MediaPark was the central element – an architectural anchor including the "Innovation Gallery" that presented the latest digital innovations, such as the AR laptop with a virtual 100-inch screen and the AI-supported testimonial "Judy".

In addition, visitors could go on a digital journey of discovery through Cologne – in formats such as guided tours, drone soccer, the first robot-human flash mob and the many brand houses of the partner companies.

Auch der begleitende DIGITAL X Summit adressierte mit Panels und Beiträgen zentrale Themen wie digitale Souveränität, künstliche Intelligenz und digitale Kompetenz. Die Inhalte wurden über sechs kuratierte Bühnen entlang der vier Megatrends vertieft: Security, Sustainability, Future of Work und Connected Business. Zu den prominenten Gästen gehörten Bundestrainer Julian Nagelsmann, Nico Rosberg, Dirk Nowitzki, die Signal-Präsidentin und AI-Forscherin Meredith Whittaker und der NRW-Ministerpräsident Hendrik Wüst.

Am Abend luden kölsche Bands auf verschiedenen Bühnen zum entspannten Ausklang ein. Ein Highlight war der Telekom Street Gig der Fantastischen Vier.

The accompanying DIGITAL X Summit also addressed key topics such as digital sovereignty, artificial intelligence and digital competence through panels and contributions. More in-depth content on the four megatrends of security, sustainability, future of work and connected business was provided by means of six curated stages. The high-profile guests included the national football trainer Julian Nagelsmann, Nico Rosberg, Dirk Nowitzki, the Signal President and AI researcher Meredith Whittaker and the NRW premier Hendrik Wüst.

In the evening, bands from Cologne on various stages invited visitors to enjoy a relaxing end to the day. One of the highlights was the Telekom Street gig by Die Fantastischen Vier.

125 YEARS DFB CEREMONY
INDUSTRIAL THEATER, KARLSRUHE

Location
Kongresshalle am Zoo, Leipzig

Client
Deutscher Fußball-Bund e.V. (DFB), Frankfurt am Main

Month / Year
January 2025

Duration
1 day

Conception / Design / Artistic production
Industrial Theater, Karlsruhe

Project lead
DFB Roland Gerfin, Frankfurt am Main

Overall artistic direction / Performance design
Enno-Ilka Uhde, Karlsruhe

Dramaturgy / Coordination
Industrial Theater Mirka Uhde, Karlsruhe

Virtual design / Videomapping
in nihilo Maria Spahn, Berlin; überraum S.A.R.L. Kai von Ahlefeld, Paris

Technology / Construction
ORANGE PRODUCTION DG GmbH & Co. KG, Blumberg (Technical supervision); FRONTSOUND Veranstaltungstechnik GmbH, Leipzig (Event technology); Wilhelm & Willhalm event technology GmbH & Co. KG, Aschheim (Light & Sound operation)

Artists / Show acts
Michael Steinbrecher (Moderation); Arnd Zeigler (Show "Mein DFB"); Daniela Vega (Mezzosoprano); Wilhelm Schwinghammer / Liangliang Zhao (Bass); Hsu-Chen Su (Piano); Anastasiia Monasypova / Vasily Bystrov (Violoncello); Martin Bosse-Platière (Flutes); Shinichi Minami (Percussion); Simon Bayne (DJ)

Photos
DFB Yuliia Perekopaiko / Thomas Böcker, Frankfurt am Main

Der Festakt zum 125-jährigen Bestehen des DFB versammelte 400 nationale und internationale Gäste, darunter Bundeskanzler Scholz, UEFA-Präsident Ceferin, FIFA-Präsident Infantino, Vertreter:innen der Vereine und Fußballverbände des In- und Auslands sowie zahlreiche Fußballlegenden.

Für die Inszenierung des Jubiläums verwandelte das Team von Industrial Theater unter der Regie von Enno-Ilka Uhde die Leipziger Kongresshalle in eine atmosphärische Fußballarena. Projektionen auf den Saalwänden, Mapping auf den Seitenbalkonen und Stadionsounds schufen eine ganzheitliche Atmosphäre. Über der Zentralbühne schwebte ein objekthafter Rundscreen, der Livebilder, 3D-Animationen und Filmzuspielungen in Szene setzte.

A CELEBRATION IS STAGED DRAMATURGICALLY AND SPATIALLY AS A FOOTBALL MATCH.

The celebration of the 125-year anniversary of DFB brought together 400 national and international guests, including Federal Chancellor Scholz, UEFA President Ceferin, FIFA President Infantino, representatives of clubs and football associations at home and abroad, as well as numerous football legends.

EIN FESTAKT WIRD DRAMATURGISCH UND RÄUMLICH ALS FUSSBALLSPIEL INSZENIERT.

The team at Industrial Theater, under the direction of Enno-Ilka Uhde, transformed the Leipzig Congress Hall into an atmospheric football arena as a setting for the celebration. Projections on the hall walls, mapping on the side balconies and stadium sounds created an immersive atmosphere. An imposing round screen floating above the central stage showed live images, 3D animations and film extracts.

Der Festakt folgte dem dramaturgischen Aufbau eines Fußballspiels: Eröffnet mit der DFB-Hymne, angepfiffen von einem Jungschiedsrichter und begleitet von einer musikalischen Performance. Eine elfköpfige Formation aus klassischen Musiker:innen und einem Stadion-DJ ließen Klassik, Pop, Livegesang und Instrumentalmusik mit Soundtracks, Torjubel und Fangesängen zu einem mitreißenden Klangbild verschmelzen.

The celebration followed the dramaturgical structure of a football match: It opened with the DFB hymn, the starting whistle was blown by a young referee and it was accompanied by a musical performance. A formation of eleven protagonists – classical musicians and a stadium DJ – made classical and pop music, live singing and instrumental music merge with soundtracks, goal celebrations and fans singing as a captivating soundscape.

TV-Journalist Arnd Zeigler und Moderator Michael Steinbrecher setzten kurzweilige Akzente. In seiner Rede thematisierte DFB-Präsident Neuendorf sowohl die glanzvollen als auch die düsteren, beschämenden Kapitel der Verbandsgeschichte. Kurz vor dem offiziellen Abschluss erklang – wie im Stadion – die deutsche Nationalhymne, begleitet von großflächigen Projektionen von Text und Nationalfarben.

TV journalist Arnd Zeigler and moderator Michael Steinbrecher provided entertaining interludes. In his speech, DFB President Neuendorf addressed both the glorious and the bleak, embarrassing chapters of the association's history. Just before the official conclusion, the German national hymn rang out – like at a stadium – accompanied by large-scale projections of texts and national colours.

minilu's
pink
fifteen
Boris Entrup
minilu.de
Dentsply
Sirona
VDW
MAILLEFER

LOGIMAT 2024

SOLIDSENSE GMBH, STUTTGART

Location
Messe Stuttgart

Client
Jungheinrich AG, Hamburg

Month / Year
March 2024

Duration
Several days

Direction / Coordination
SOLIDSENSE GmbH, Stuttgart

Architecture / Design
AMT – Agentur für Markenträume GmbH, Esslingen; SOLIDSENSE GmbH, Stuttgart

Construction
SOLIDSENSE GmbH, Stuttgart; Neumann&Müller GmbH & Co. KG, Stuttgart

Others
pool3 GmbH – Technische Animationen & VR Systeme, Niederwaldkirchen; wirmachenbunt GmbH & Co. KG, Hamburg

Photos
Andreas Keller, Altdorf; Markus Burkhardt, Stuttgart

Auf der LogiMAT 2024 wollte sich Jungheinrich nicht nur als Anbieter von Intralogistik-Hardware, sondern zudem als umfassender Anbieter für den gesamten Bereich der Intralogistik positionieren. Die zentrale Botschaft: Jungheinrich bietet mehr als „Trucks" – es steht für eine intelligente, vernetzte Lagerwelt.

Mit einem zentralen Messestand-Element von SOLIDSENSE, AMT, Pool3 und wirmachenbunt wurde ein interaktives 3D-Modell der idealen Lagerwelt entwickelt, realisiert in einer Game Engine. An mehreren Stationen konnten Besucher:innen eigenständig das digitale Modell erkunden und die Vernetzung von Produkten, Software und Services erleben. Der Aufbau folgte einer klaren Dramaturgie: visuelle Orientierung, interaktive Vertiefung und thematische Verknüpfung über verschiedene Touchpoints. Das Centerpiece bestand je Seite aus je zwei transparenten, interaktiven OLED-Monitorflächen und einem Ultrawide Screen dahinter. Das Besondere war die Kombination aus physischen und digitalen Komponenten.

At LogiMAT 2024, Jungheinrich wanted to position themselves not only as a supplier of intralogistics hardware but also as a comprehensive supplier for the whole field of intralogistics. The central message was: Jungheinrich offers more than "trucks" – it stands for an intelligent, networked warehouse world.

AN INTERACTIVE 3D MODEL MAKES IT POSSIBLE TO EXPERIENCE A NETWORKED WAREHOUSE WORLD PHYSICALLY AND DIGITALLY.

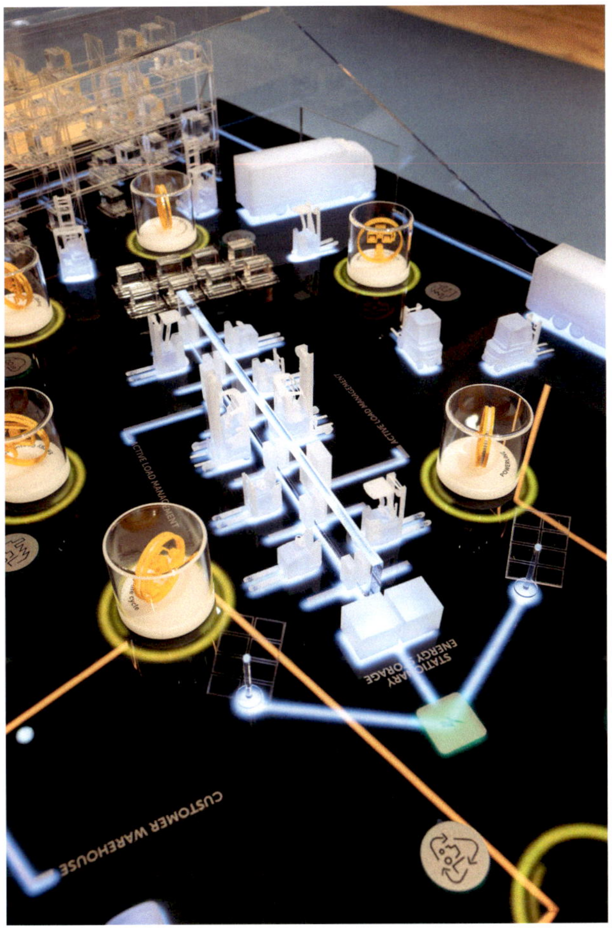

EIN INTERAKTIVES 3D-MODELL MACHT EINE VERNETZTE LAGERWELT PHYSISCH UND DIGITAL ERFAHRBAR.

With a central exhibition stand element by SOLIDSENSE, AMT, Pool3 and wirmachenbunt, an interactive 3D model of an ideal warehouse world was developed and realised in a game engine. Visitors were able to explore the digital model independently at several stations and experience the networking of products, software and services. The structure followed a clear dramaturgy: visual orientation, interactive insights and thematic linking through various touchpoints. The centrepiece consisted of two transparent, interactive OLED monitor surfaces on each side respectively and an ultrawide screen behind it. The special feature was the combination of physical and digital components.

Interaktionen per Touch auf der vorderen, transparenten OLED-Ebene beeinflussten die Contentebene dahinter, wobei Inhalte zwischen den Ebenen sprangen. Zusätzlich wurden per AR kontextbezogene Inhalte auf das physische Lagermodell gemappt. Alle vier Seiten des Centerpiece waren inhaltlich synchronisiert und in die 3D-Welt eingebunden.

Eine Herausforderung war die Umsetzung der gelayerten Monitorebenen sowie die technische Integration der Touchfunktion über zwei transparente OLED-Displays hinweg. Um Moiré-Effekte zu vermeiden, waren präzise Abstimmungen nötig. Auch die statische Konstruktion mit großen Überhängen und geringen Toleranzen stellte hohe Ansprüche an Planung und Fertigung. Ergänzt wurde das Centerpiece durch fünf Satelliten-Stelen, abgestimmt auf einzelne Produktbereiche. Sie verlängerten das Erlebnis an weitere Positionen des Standes.

Interactions through touch on the front transparent OLED level influenced the content level behind it, whereby content jumped back and forth between the levels. In addition, context-related content was mapped on the physical warehouse model using AR. All four sides of the centrepiece were synchronised in terms of content and incorporated into the 3D world.

One of the challenges was realising the layered monitor levels, as well as the technical integration of the touch function through two transparent OLED displays. Precise coordination was necessary in order to avoid moiré effects. The structural construction with large overhangs and low tolerances was very demanding on planning and manufacturing. The centrepiece was supplemented by five satellite steles, coordinated with the individual product ranges. They extended the experience to further positions on the stand.

T Systems
ORCHES TRATING A NEW ERA
AI POWERED
aws Amazon Web Services
Connected Table Football
YOUR AI LIVE PORTRAIT
WANNA LOOK LIKE A STAR?
LET'S DO IT!
T Systems
ORCHES RATING A NEW ERA
ORCHES TRATING A NEW ERA

ORCHESTRATING A NEW ERA

PHOCUS BRAND CONTACT GMBH & CO. KG, NUREMBERG

Location
25hours Hotel The Circle, Cologne

Client
T-Systems International GmbH, Frankfurt am Main

Month / Year
September 2024

Duration
2 days

Dramaturgy
PHOCUS BRAND CONTACT
Anja Osswald / Volker Hagen, Nuremberg

Direction / Coordination
PHOCUS BRAND CONTACT
Anja Häberle, Nuremberg

Architecture / Design
PHOCUS BRAND CONTACT
Eva Köhler, Nuremberg

Graphics
PHOCUS BRAND CONTACT
Mareike Voss / Felix Schmidt, Nuremberg

Lighting
Michael Wirtz GmbH, Cologne;
Aventem GmbH Marko Paulussen, Hilden

Media
Michael Wirtz GmbH, Cologne;
PHOCUS BRAND CONTACT
Maximilian Oschmann, Nuremberg

Films
Raphael Duschek, Cologne; DECAID Studio Timo Springer / Felix Leber, Berlin

Artists / Show acts
EVENTCOMEDY Die Pagen, Cologne;
Christian Schulte-Loh, Cologne

Decoration
BALLONI GmbH Rebecca Nolden, Cologne

Catering
Restaurant NENI Köln, Cologne

Others
DECAID Studio Timo Springer / Felix Leber, Berlin (AI applications)

Photos
Gesa Niessen, music4friends, Cologne

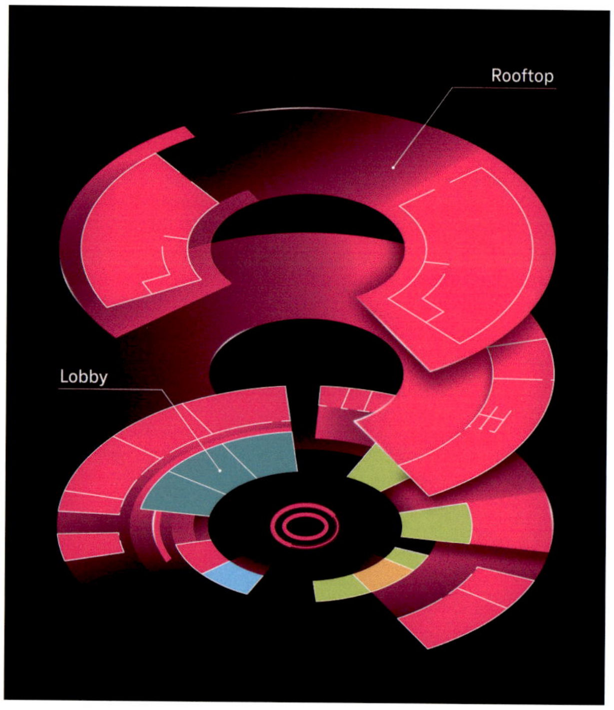

Künstliche Intelligenz ist eines der zentralen Themen der digitalen Transformation. Doch wie kann ihr volles Potenzial entfaltet und ein echter Mehrwert geschaffen werden? Diese Fragen standen im Mittelpunkt der T-Systems-Präsenz auf der DIGITAL X 2024. Nach drei Jahren auf dem Digital Festival setzte sich T-Systems das Ziel, das Brandhouse zu einer der meistbesuchten Locations zu befördern. Unter dem Motto „Orchestrating a new era" entstand ein Erlebnisraum, der Technologie, Interaktion und Markenpräsenz verband.

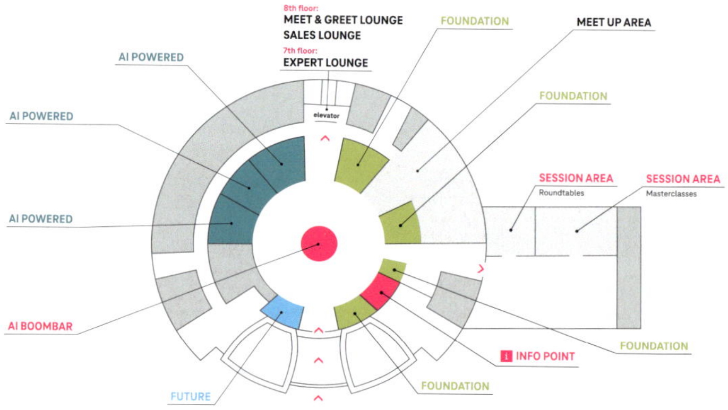

A BRAND HOUSE THAT COMBINES TECHNOLOGY, INTERACTION AND BRAND PRESENCE AS AN IMMERSIVE EXPERIENCE.

Artificial intelligence is one of the central topics of the digital transformation. How can its full potential be unleashed in order to create true added value? Such questions were at the heart of the T-Systems presence at DIGITAL X 2024. After three years at the Digital Festival, T-Systems set itself the goal of making its brand house to one of the most highly frequented locations. The result was a spatial experience that combined technology, interaction and brand presence, under the motto of "orchestrating a new era".

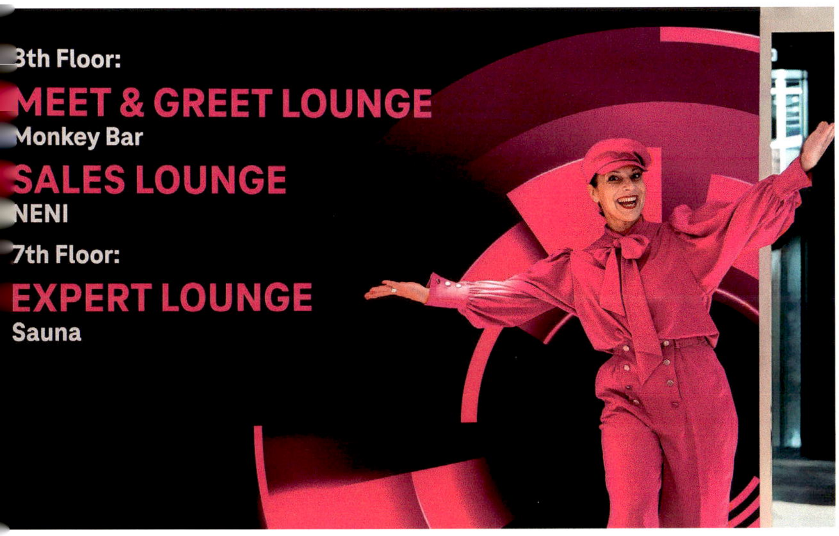

PHOCUS BRAND CONTACT entwickelte für das Brandhouse ein Konzept, das die ikonische Architektur des denkmalgeschützten 25hours Hotel The Circle mit dem Versprechen von T-Systems vereinte: Technologien und Lösungen harmonisch miteinander zu verknüpfen. Über mehrere Etagen hinweg boten Sessions, Showcases, Live-Demos und persönliche Gespräche ein ganzheitliches Erlebnis. Vom imposanten Erdgeschoss mit Ausstellungs- und Partnerbereich bis hin zu exklusiven Networking-Formaten im oberen Stockwerk – selbst der Spabereich wurde zur Expert Lounge umgestaltet.

PHOCUS BRAND CONTACT developed a concept for the brand house that merged the iconic, heritage-listed architecture of the 25hours Hotel The Circle with T-Systems' promise: the harmonious combination of technologies and solutions. Sessions, showcases, live demos and one-on-one-conversations spread over several floors offered a holistic experience. From the impressive ground floor with its exhibition and partner area to exclusive networking formats on the top floor – even the spa area was converted into an expert lounge.

EIN BRANDHOUSE, DAS TECHNOLOGIE, INTERAKTION UND MARKENPRÄSENZ ALS GANZHEIT-LICHES ERLEBNIS VERBINDET.

Ein Highlight war die AI BoomBar, die als inhaltlicher Dreh- und Angelpunkt für digitale Lösungen fungierte und die gesamte Location prägte. Sie symbolisierte das Zusammenspiel zwischen Mensch und künstlicher Intelligenz und schuf eine inspirierende Plattform für Austausch.

Digitale Inszenierungen, wiederverwendbares Branding, eine intelligente Nutzung der bestehenden Hotelarchitektur sowie kulinarische Highlights aus der hauseigenen NENI-Küche rundeten das Konzept ab. Mit über 12.000 Besucher:innen war das T-Systems Brandhouse eine der meistfrequentierten Locations auf der DIGITAL X 2024.

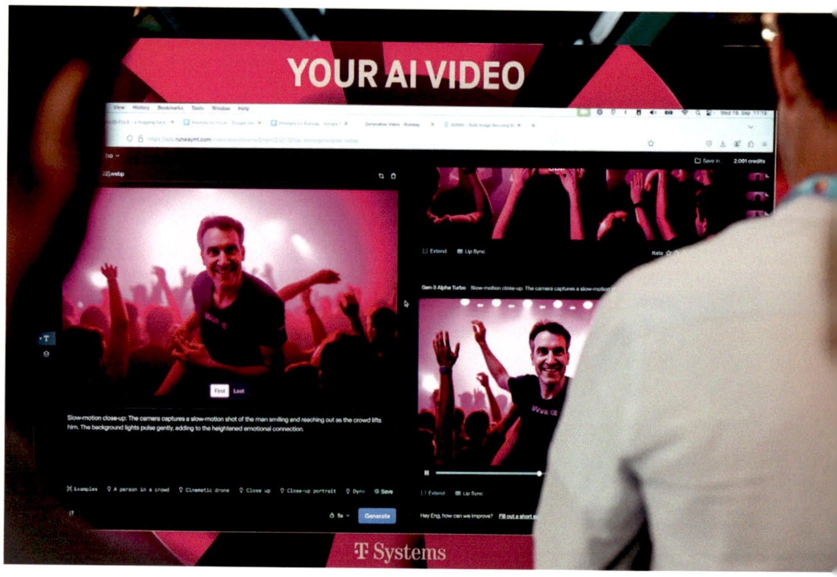

The AI BoomBar was a highlight, acting as a thematic hub for digital solutions, and set the tone for the entire location. It symbolised the interplay of humans and artificial intelligence, creating an inspiriring platform for exchange.

Digital settings, reusable branding, intelligent use of the existing hotel architecture and culinary highlights from the in-house NENI kitchen rounded off the concept. With over 12,000 visitors, the T-Systems brandhouse was one of the most frequented locations at DIGITAL X 2024.

Ihr setzt Erlebnisdesign als Form des künstlerischen Protests ein. Warum Live-Aktionen? Was können „echte" Erlebnisse, was andere Formate nicht können?

Echte Erlebnisse generieren authentische Geschichten und Bilder. Sie führen insbesondere beim Adenauer SRP+ zu Dynamiken, die oftmals nicht oder nur bedingt vorhersehbar sind. Wie verläuft der Protest, wie reagieren die Faschist:innen der AfD, was macht die Polizei, welche Position bezieht die (demokratische) Politik und was berichten Medien?

Die Protagonisten entscheiden eigenständig über ihr Handeln und beeinflussen damit, teilweise auch eher unfreiwillig, die Geschichte. So konnten wir etwa beim AfD-Parteitag in Riesa stundenlang die Hauptzufahrt der Abgeordneten blockieren, weil ein Beamter der Polizei „kurz pinkeln" musste. Ein Augenblick des zivilen Ungehorsams, 500 Meter Verfolgungsjagd und dann eine Panne mitten auf der Kreuzung. Schade! Durch wirklichen Zufall war genau in diesem Moment Spiegel TV an Bord. Der Polizist hat also eher unfreiwillig dabei geholfen, unsere Forderung sichtbarer zu machen, und die Geschichte mitgeschrieben.

MAN KANN SICH EINIGES VORHER AUSDENKEN, WAS ABER WIRKLICH PASSIERT, IST VON GANZ VIELEN UNPLANBAREN FAKTOREN ABHÄNGIG.

Das macht es spannend. Für alle Beteiligten.

Der Adenauer SRP+ ist ein umgebauter Bus – als mobile Bühne, Ausstellung und Barrikade. Was steckt inhaltlich dahinter?

Wir fordern ein AfD-Verbotsverfahren und das braucht Mehrheiten in der Politik. Seit über zehn Jahren behaupten Politiker:innen, die AfD inhaltlich stellen oder gar durch eine Zusammenarbeit „entzaubern" zu können. Die AfD ist aktuell stärkste Kraft und jetzt als „gesichert rechtsextreme" Partei bestätigt! Wir sehen in einem Verbot den einzig wirkungsvollen Weg, die AfD noch rechtzeitig zu bekämpfen. Wir warten nicht weiter! Wir machen Druck, wir mobilisieren und wir aktivieren. Entschlossen und bereit zu kämpfen. Ohne Weichspülparolen, die jeden mitnehmen, sondern stattdessen klar und deutlich: Die AfD ist eine Nazipartei. Punkt. Der Adenauer wurde von weit über 10.000 Investoren finanziert und es werden täglich mehr.

Wie kann auch die Live-Kommunikation ihr Fachwissen nutzen, um Verantwortung zu übernehmen und sich politisch zu engagieren? Und warum sollte sie das tun?

Die AfD kommuniziert skrupellos und erfolgreich – mit Lügen, Hetze und Manipulation. Und die Kommunikationsbranche kann bzw. könnte deutlich dazu beitragen, entschieden dagegen vorzugehen. Sie verfügt über die notwendigen Werkzeuge, das Netzwerk und die Fähigkeiten, wirkungsvoll zu kommunizieren. Für Geld inszeniert die Welt der Werbung jeden Kram, aber für gesellschaftliche Themen ist leider keine Zeit. Wann sollte man das auch alles noch tun?!

Wir müssen endlich aufhören zu glauben, es würden sich schon andere kümmern. Die AfD ist aktuell stärkste Kraft. Was braucht es noch, damit wir mehr als einmal im Jahr auf die Straße gehen und demonstrieren?

Ja – ihr seid gemeint!

ERLEBNISDESIGN ALS PROTEST
EXPERIENCE DESIGN AS A PROTEST
INTERVIEW WITH ARNE HEYEN (ZENTRUM FÜR POLITISCHE SCHÖNHEIT)

You use experience design as a form of artistic protest. Why live campaigns? What can "real" experiences do that other formats cannot?

Real experiences generate authentic stories and images. They lead especially for the Adenauer SRP+ to dynamics that are often not foreseeable, or only to a limited extent. How does the protest unfold, how do the fascists of AfD react, what are the police doing, what stance does (democratic) politics take and what do the media report?

The protagonists decide independently regarding their actions and thereby influence the story, sometimes also rather involuntarily. For example, at the AfD party conference in Riesa, we were able to block the main access of the AfD delegates for hours, because a police offer had to "have a quick pee". A brief moment of civil disobedience, 500 metres of pursuit and then a breakdown in the middle of the crossing. A pity! By pure coincidence, just at that moment Spiegel TV was at the scene. The policeman therefore helped rather involuntarily to make our demands more visible and co-write the story.

ONE CAN PLAN A LOT BEFOREHAND, BUT WHAT REALLY HAPPENS DEPENDS ON MANY FACTORS THAT CAN'T BE PLANNED.

That makes it interesting. For all those involved.

The Adenauer SRP+ is a converted bus – as a mobile stage, exhibition and barricade. What is behind it in terms of content?

We are calling for an AfD prohibition procedure and this requires majorities in politics. Politicians have been claiming for over ten years that they can challenge AfD in terms of content or "break their spell" through cooperation. AfD is currently the strongest power and has now been officially confirmed as a "right-wing extremist" party! For us, a prohibition is the only effective way to combat the AfD in time. We are not waiting any longer! We are exerting pressure, we are mobilising and activating. We are decisive and ready to fight. Without soft talk but instead loud and clear: AfD is a Nazi party. Full stop. The Adenauer was financed by way over 10,000 investors and there are more every day.

How can live communication also use its expert knowledge to assume responsibility and become politically involved? And why should it do so?

AfD communicates without scruples and successfully – with lies, agitation and manipulation. And the communication sector can or could contribute significantly to taking decisive action against it. It has the necessary tools, the network and the capabilities to communicate effectively. The world of advertising puts forth any rubbish for money, but unfortunately there is no time for social issues. How is one supposed to manage it all?!

We must finally stop believing that others will take care of it. AfD is currently the strongest power. What more does it take for us to take to the streets more than once a year and demonstrate?

Yes – it's you we're talking to!

Photo: Zentrum für Politische Schönheit

Arne Heyen, Zentrum für Politische Schönheit
www.politicalbeauty.de

IMPRESSUM
IMPRINT

Author	Katharina Stein
Editing / Setting	Mario Ableitner
Translation	Lynne Kolar-Thompson
Layout	Tina Agard Grafik & Buchdesign, Esslingen / Neckar
Lithography	Paladin Design- und Werbemanufaktur, Remseck
Printing	Printed by GPS in Bosnia & Herzegowina
Paper	Condat matt Périgord / 170 g/m²
Cover photo	flora&faunavisions GmbH, Berlin Utopian Garden
Image recognition	www.ayscan.de

Publishing and Manufacturing

avedition GmbH
Publishers for Architecture and Design
Dr. Petra Kiedaisch
Senefelderstr. 109
70176 Stuttgart
Germany
Tel.: +49 (0)711 / 220 22 79-0
Fax: +49 (0)711 / 220 22 79-15
eventdesign@avedition.de
www.avedition.com

ISBN 978-3-89986-432-8

Redaktioneller Hinweis:
In einigen Fällen haben wir auf geschlechtsspezifische Begriffe verzichtet, um das Lesen zu vereinfachen. Falls wir die männliche Form von personenbezogenen Hauptwörtern gewählt haben, ist damit keine Herabwürdigung und / oder Diskriminierung andersgeschlechtlicher Personen beabsichtigt.